BEST PRACTICES OF THE BUSINESS PRESS

A Resource
for Mastering Business-to-Business,
Trade, and Association Publication Editing

American Society of Business Publication Editors

Robert Freedman, Editor

D0521566

KENDALL/HUNT PUBLISHING COMPANY
4050 Westmark Drive   Dubuque, Iowa 52002

CONTENTS

Introduction

In the Beginning Was an
Article on Tap Fittings

The business press has a simple mission: to help people in their profession. It's this service journalism aspect of the business press that sets it apart from the consumer press and constitutes the standard by which the performance of business publication editors are measured. As an editor, you can strive to inform and entertain your readers. But can you help them?

To be sure, consumer publications want to help their readers, too. It wasn't too long ago that *The Wall Street Journal* launched its "Weekend Journal" and then a little later its "Personal Journal." Here's my take on the intent of those two sections: to provide the same in-depth coverage on the fun side of money (the spending of it) that *The Wall Street Journal* is known for on the serious side (the earning of it). But there's a twist: the coverage is heavily weighted toward service journalism. For the *Journal,* it's not enough to report that husbands and wives are increasingly installing his-and-her bathrooms in their home (an article in its August 15, 2003, issue). That kind of coverage is merely news. What takes the coverage to the level of service journalism is the information intended to help you, the reader, act on what's being reported. Are you thinking about installing his-and-her bathrooms in your house, too? Here's how much you can expect to spend, and here are the issues you can expect to confront.

The service journalism in the business press isn't typically as fun as it is in *The Wall Street Journal*. If you think of coverage of an issue as something of a food chain, with "his-and-her bathrooms" at the top of the chain, then *The Wall Street Journal* has pride of place. The editors can talk about the funny things consumers are doing and have a good time doing it. But before *The Wall Street Journal* can take its cut at the issue, scores of trade publications must do their thing. Magazines in the construction industry must write about why remodelers are going for honed stone countertops rather than flamed granite, and what the tricks are of mastering installation; magazines in the engineering industries must write about the benefits of polypropylene piping compared to polyethylene piping, and where the best sources are for each; and magazines in the design industries must write about the excitement over square tap fittings, and how they're being fitted to solve styling problems.

Although the service journalism in the trade press only occasionally is presented with the jazziness of *The Wall Street Journal's* "Weekend Journal" or "Personal Journal," it has one thing going for it that its cousins in the consumer press won't necessarily have: a central role in the exchange of best practices within a business or industry. It's this exchange of best practices that makes industries and professions dynamic.

In fact, sharing best practices is what this book is all about. Business publication editing is a profession, too, and editors exchange best practices as they seek to improve the usefulness of their publications to their readers. Editors attend conferences and talk with one another to collect ideas on how to design publications, plan content, organize departments, and research, write, assign, edit, and present articles—and everything else they do. That's what the exchange of best practices is all about.

And that's where this publication comes in. The essays in this collection are from editors who practice the craft of business publication editing every day, and from educators whose roots are in the business press. All of the contributors are either members of the American Society of Business Publication Editors, academics, or editors whose work has been recognized by ASBPE for its editorial or design excellence. ASBPE is a 40-year-old nonprofit organization whose members are editors of business publications throughout the United States. The Society hosts the country's largest awards program for recognizing editorial and design excellence in the business press (almost 2,300 entries in 2003), and offers workshops, conference sessions, panel discussions, and other programs for enhancing business press editors' professional skills. It also conducts surveys on key issues in the profession, and provides resources for editors at its Web site, *www.asbpe.org*.

Like the ASBPE programs, the focus of this publication is on the practical. What's the best way to cover a trade show? What are the steps for launching a publication? What makes for hard-hitting business reporting? How do you redesign a publication to enhance the user-benefit of articles? What makes an effective how-to article? How do you approach design with an eye toward enhancing the service journalism aspect of your coverage?

The essays won't provide all the answers. But they may provoke questions and give you ideas, and in that way provide you with information that's useful—which is what the business press is all about.

Robert Freedman
Washington, D.C.

Personal Reflection

Knowing an Ingot from an Extrusion

*Trade publications have learned from the consumer side of journalism—
but without giving an inch on their mastery of the arcane.*

Roy J. Harris, Jr.

Change has swept through the world of trade publications. The so-called trades, or business publications, are far more attractively designed than they were a decade ago, and increasingly resemble newsstand cousins such as *BusinessWeek, Fortune, SmartMoney, Inc.,* and *Forbes.* Sometimes, in fact, the trades look better.

The biggest change in the trades, though, has been in editorial quality. We live in an ironic era, when a glut of business information can obstruct the availability of intelligent insight about individual business lines. To survive, trades must provide that targeted insight in a meaningful way. No longer can they be the one-dimensional compilations of company and association press releases that some once were. Their own business is, for want of a better expression, "news you can use"—articles crafted to transfer to readers the special knowledge that magazine staffers acquire about what's important to readers in a particular field. And while this knowledge often takes the form of news summaries or short how-to items, it also resides in the in-depth, interpretative coverage of major issues that's now a hallmark of many trade publications.

The business press has honed its skills by adopting reportorial and editing techniques pioneered by the best general-circulation magazines and newspapers. Many trade publications have hired staff with experience writing for broader audiences—staffers who now employ a range of story styles tailored to the information being dispensed in the feature well of trade magazines. And this, too, has drawn readers into their pages, exposing larger audiences to significant issues.

The magazine I write and edit for, *CFO,* exemplifies this new breed of trade publication. The 18-year-old Boston-based monthly now has 450,000 subscribers—nearly every corporate finance executive in the United States. In 2003, *CFO* was named the top trade magazine by the American Society of Business Publication Editors in part for its work exploring the accounting scandals that engulfed the U.S. in 2001 and 2002.

CFO began establishing its reputation for pursuing meaty issue-based stories from its beginning, but it took its reporting to a new level after its purchase in 1989 by The Economist Group, publisher of *The Economist.* That's not to say the magazine didn't

Roy J. Harris, Jr., a former reporter with The Wall Street Journal, *is senior editor of* CFO, *published by The Economist Group, in Boston.*

sometimes miss the forest for the trees. As *CFO* founding editor Julia Homer says, its early years were sometimes a little soft, dedicated to stories about "CFOs doing a good job at a good company." With the help of its British owners, though, *CFO* gained focus. It began aggressively hiring, looking for the experienced, knowledgeable, and passionate journalists that are key to producing ambitious stories. The revitalized staff, backed by the *Economist's* strong culture of quality and independence, bolstered Homer's contention that in order to compete effectively for ad dollars, *CFO* should be at least as good as its competitors in the general press.

Today, in Homer's view, the business press has improved so much that passing up a major story in a magazine's coverage area isn't an option. "If an issue is out there and the trade magazine tries to ignore it," she says, "it looks like an idiot."

After a 23-year career at *The Wall Street Journal,* I signed on as *CFO* senior editor in 1996. I had discovered the trade press upon joining the *Journal* in 1971, just out of the Army and journalism graduate school. Assigned to my first business beat in Pittsburgh, I was trying to keep up with a quartet of *Journal* veterans who knew the wide assortment of companies the bureau covered, including then-powerhouses like U.S. Steel and Alcoa, Gulf Oil, Westinghouse, H.J. Heinz, and Mellon Bank. Supposedly, I had the easiest beat in the office: aluminum. Still, it all seemed intimidating, especially since I knew that nearly two million readers wanted top-flight coverage from the paper—and had a right to expect that its aluminum reporter would know an ingot from an extrusion.

The metals-industry magazines the *Journal* subscribed to—big titles included *American Metal Market, Metalworking News,* and *Iron Age*—were a godsend. While largely collections of straight news and industry trend stories, and dry as bauxite, they were full of ideas. Buried in their columns, for example, was the determination of aluminum-makers to increase its usage in automobiles, to become the metal of choice in soda and beer cans, and even to replace wood in baseball bats. And in a related pursuit, aluminum was seeking to change its image from energy hog to environmental savior. (Recycling in the early '70s was nearly unheard-of, and the metal was known for the huge amounts of power required to produce it, and for its persistence as litter, never rusting away, as steel cans did.) Clearly, its drive for new markets held great interest for *Journal* readers as well.

Four years later, I moved to the Los Angeles bureau, taking over the aerospace and defense beat and inheriting a different set of trades. The aviation press—led by McGraw Hill's "bible of aerospace," *Aviation Week & Space Technology*—was more ambitious and better written. *Av Week,* for one, loved to break stories that the *Journal* and others would have to follow. For any entertainment stories that came my way, the *Hollywood Reporter* and *Variety* served well. The latter was best-known, perhaps, for telling readers that "Hix Nix Stix Pix" (translation: small-town moviegoers shun shows about small towns). But *Variety* also was, and is, adept at exploring movie-industry spending scandals and contract disputes that later became fodder for the broader consumer press. It was thus "must" reading in our office. When covering a *Journal* beat, in fact, the trades are as much a part of the regular reading regimen as are *BusinessWeek* and *Fortune*. Reporters often draw on sources from their trades, and quickly learn that people quoted in a trade book may be even more eager to chat when they might get their names in a general-circulation publication.

Angering Advertisers: A Test of the Soul

Business journalists are hardly the major audience for trade publications, of course. Examining the connection between these two sectors of journalism, though, sheds a valuable light on the vital role of trades in the media. And a look at techniques for issued-based coverage that the top specialty magazines have adopted from the consumer press certainly helps explain how the once-huge quality gap has closed between the business media and its general-circulation counterparts.

San Francisco-based *PC World,* which has grown into a 6.9-million circulation giant for specialist-magazine publisher IDG, has always viewed itself "at its heart, as a publication about products," editor Harry McCracken says. "But more and more we've discovered that this doesn't mean that investigative reporting and reader advocacy and good, old-fashioned muckraking are beyond our scope. As a matter of fact they're increasingly essential." In addition to product-based investigations, *PC World* has been taking aim at the Web lately. "The Internet has more than its share of shady merchants, privacy violators, and other ne'er-do-wells. So we publish investigative reports on topics such as online merchants and advertisers."

Obviously, a trade magazine's narrower coverage area can be a breeding ground for conflict if some of the relative handful of powerful industry forces, including advertisers, react negatively to tough reporting. And trade publications are particularly vulnerable to such pressure in economic downturns, when angry advertisers could hurt revenues by pulling out of the publication. This is where a magazine's soul can be tested.

"From time to time we've lost advertising when articles have said unflattering things about technology companies," says *PC World's* McCracken. "But readers tell us again and again that they appreciate hard-hitting reporting, and can tell that we're on their side. And many of these stories have won us editorial awards." *CFO* agrees that today's specialty magazine benefits from showing backbone in the reader's service. "Advertisers are sophisticated enough to understand that they can't expect a trade magazine to turn a blind eye to problems, any more than they would expect *Fortune* or *Forbes* to do so," says Julia Homer. "Nonetheless, criticizing an advertiser is always a sensitive issue. These days, we ensure that the criticism is valid and confirmed by several sources. We give the advertiser the opportunity to state its position on the issue, and we let the publisher know in advance if a story will be critical. He can then make the judgment about whether to hold a particular ad, or let it run."

A Personal Connection: The Trade Magazine's Draw

A word about the value of a close-knit, collegial staff in pursuing broad issue-based stories: trade publications have learned to see their special connection with readers—a bond much like that shared by local newspapers, newsletters, and online publications with the narrow "communities" they reach—as a unique advantage. Their ability to use that connection to respond to reader needs creates reader loyalty, a quality that advertisers especially prize. But as the magazine staff itself forms its bond with readers, there is a valuable by-product: the collaborative feeling in the office, as reporters and editors share similar goals for coverage that meets readers' needs. And whatever the size of the staff, there is no substitute for the support of one's co-workers in the pursuit of major stories.

Joining *CFO* in 1996, I discovered camaraderie among its dozen-or-so staffers that quite resembled the spirit in my old *Wall Street Journal* bureaus in Pittsburgh and L.A. The spirit translated into strong coverage for readers. And not coincidentally, I believe, *CFO,* like the *Journal,* enjoys fantastic subscriber loyalty. To meet a *CFO* reader is to find an enthusiast.

In a personal sense, I understand this draw of the trade magazine, for I've always been attracted to specialized publications in my own field of journalism. No matter how compelling the cover of *Fortune* might be, I'll read *Columbia Journalism Review* or *Folio:* first if the lead story offers insights into my chosen profession and the life of an editor. Over the years, I've learned to approach writing for *CFO* readers the same way—with a desire to deal intelligently with the issues that grip them day-to-day, personalizing the focus in a way the general media can't.

What separates an "issue" from just another story? Usually, its scope; a major issue is simply a topic that is on many readers' minds—one that is characterized by many points of view, with some degree of passion connected to each.

The issue-based *CFO* stories considered in this chapter deal with corporate finance: managing conflicts with other top executives, customer reactions to flaws in a popular software product, educational shortcomings in the training delivered by universities, the question of how drug money can find its way to corporate bottom lines, and, of course, the finance scandals and reforms that have dominated our coverage in recent years. But lessons from the preparation of these articles apply to nearly every trade magazine, whether its audience is made up of accountants, computer technicians, morticians, truckers, or veterinarians.

What's the Big Idea? From Issue to Feature Well

Ideas for articles about the major issues confronting readers can come from all over, of course—from formal reader surveys or suggestions, from magazine advisory boards, from comments made by your sources on other stories, from grains of information in company press releases, or from stories that other magazines or newspapers simply failed to cover with the level of detail your readers required. And the ways you can choose to present your article to readers are at least as diverse. But before selecting your topic, and the style with which to write about it, some basic guidelines can help improve your chances for a powerful, high-quality project.

1. *Do some preliminary idea formation.* Discuss the issue in a formal editorial story meeting, or bounce it off other editors on your own. Look for new angles

to the story, and note the places where you will have to find balancing viewpoints. Get feedback, too, from industry sources you trust—using discretion, though, and realizing that sources have a way of passing ideas around, including to other media. Then, crystallize the issue in a short paragraph. You need to have confidence that your issue is solid and really new to readers. Do a thorough Web or library search to see what others have written on the topic, and what your own publication might have said about it, perhaps years earlier. (This may allow you to make historical references that give your story more depth, while celebrating the past work of your magazine.)

2. *Start building a diverse source list.* To your initial sources, add names of people you think could contribute to all sides of a story, striking them off only as they fail to deliver. In an industry story, remember that competitors, customers, suppliers, Wall Street analysts, consultants, and academics, among others, all may be useful. And that's just a starting point. The list should grow rapidly as you make your first calls. Along the way, ask sources who else you might talk with—including those who disagree with them.

3. *Develop techniques for winning over "difficult" sources.* When you seek balance in your article, people you interview usually get the message that you are trying to be fair. If sources do get upset, perhaps with negative material that will appear about their companies, I sometimes ask them to consider what *they* would want to read if the story were about a *competitor.* Should competitors be covered "warts and all?" Would they *believe* a report that was 100% positive? For reluctant sources, find ways to persuade them to stay on the record, because your readers want to know who is making the claims in your story. The best way may be to assure them that you will read over the quoted matter you'll be attributing to them, and that you'll give them a sense of the context in which their comments will appear. If your magazine has a fact-checking process, explain that as yet another chance to hear the gist of what is to be published.

4. *Think "reader usefulness" from day one.* Walking in the reader's shoes helps you develop new ideas, ensure balance, and devise good presentation techniques—including sidebars and meaningful graphics to illustrate the piece. Sidebars often help you keep interesting elements of a complex story from getting lost. And they give you a chance to write multiple catchy leads, instead of just one.

5. *Revisit the theme throughout the interview process.* Don't get "stuck" with your proposal. Be willing to change elements as you go along, if your reporting reflects that need. And imagine where the story might take you. Let your theme expand if that is warranted, and you can make a broader point. (IMPORTANT: Make sure you advise previous interviewees of major changes in your approach, so they're not blindsided by what the article says. When you call them back, listen for new angles that might affect your revised theme.)

6. *Remember that you are telling a story.* Even deeply analytical articles—and sometimes *especially* those—can benefit from stretches of narrative, historical

reflections, personal profiling, or other writing nuances. They can engage readers and make subjects more human. Of course, while it's great to have an original approach, make sure that the reader comes first here, too. The article's opening should draw readers in without over-promising what is to follow. And present the issue in capsule form—in the so-called nut paragraph, which often requires the most work—so that readers have a clear idea of where the story will go. From then on, the story line should be easy to follow. (NOTE: Some reporters think personality profiles carry a license to deliver their own opinions freely. In my experience, such writing actually requires *deeper* reporting—to understand the varied opinions of others, to be fair, and to avoid being simplistic.)

In examining the following stories from *CFO,* look for how these guidelines apply.

Study #1
"In-Flight Infight"—Dealing with Executive Power Struggles

My own story ideas often stem from "holes" I find in interesting news stories or feature articles published by others—and especially my old employer, the *Journal.* I love writing about personalities. So my favorite stories result when a study of personalities helps draw important business lessons for readers. In 1997, a front-page article appeared in the *Journal* about Delta Airlines' ouster of its CEO, Ron Allen. Deep in the story, it was pointed out that Allen, shortly before he himself was let go, had proposed to the board of directors the sacking of Delta CFO Thomas Roeck. While the *Journal* article had lots of interesting detail about how Allen's imperiousness had turned off directors, it said little about the deterioration of his relationship with Roeck, or why the board sided with Roeck and dismissed Allen instead. Not as compelling for the *Journal* reader, perhaps, but excellent fodder for a *CFO* article.

In a story meeting, the staff shared my curiosity about this missing personality piece in the Delta shake-up puzzle. With CFOs becoming central players at many companies, and more independent, there was increasing chance that they would clash with CEOs, who are generally the strongest individual forces in Corporate America. Almost as important, the trust that CFOs can earn with the board was another story that our audience would be eager to read about.

Delta's public relations department eagerly helped with the basics—tacitly confirming in the process that Allen had been roundly unpopular, even in P.R. But it wasn't about to elaborate on the executive spat that the *Journal* story had unearthed, or to discuss the inner-workings of the board. So while my source list started with the handful of people quoted in the *Journal*—and neither Allen nor Roeck were—I began listing board members and seeking out people from the airline's finance department. Not surprisingly, several had left the company not long before, including a former treasurer and a former risk-management head. Along with the directors, they moved to the head of my contact list.

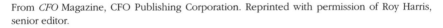

Read widely—and closely. Story ideas in the business press often come when you're not looking for them. A reference in a *Wall Street Journal* article about a clash between two Delta executives was the starting point for this high-impact *CFO* feature.

From *CFO* Magazine, CFO Publishing Corporation. Reprinted with permission of Roy Harris, senior editor.

The former Delta financial officials, in other jobs by then, had strong feelings that Roeck, their former boss, had been wronged by CEO Allen, and they had no compunctions about saying so for the record. Roeck had come to Delta via its acquisition of Western Airlines years before, and these executives painted a picture of a forthright finance chief whose legitimate warnings about problems lying ahead for Delta weren't heeded by the airline's old-timers. Among those resisting the news was Allen.

Board members—some of whom had talked to the *Journal* earlier—also chose to weigh in for the *CFO* story. And support here too was strong for the trusted CFO Roeck. Wall Street analysts also roundly liked Roeck's style, and felt that Allen couldn't grasp basic financial concepts. Gradually, a picture emerged of how the board could have sided with the finance chief, and cut the CEO loose. With each major element of the squabble that was confirmed, Delta P.R. had another chance to respond, yet generally declined.

Armed with a compelling version of the story, based on a range of opinions from both insiders and outsiders at Delta, I went back to try to get Roeck's and Allen's reactions. The two wouldn't comment. But through each step of the reporting process, a clear theme took shape: "Indeed, Allen emerges in some accounts as the classic fair-weather navigator, handy at the controls during Delta's good times, but ill-suited to see it through stormy conditions. [A] blind spot about finance . . . kept Allen from taking the prudent suggestions of a CFO experienced in dealing with adversity. And by interpreting Roeck's early warnings as symptoms of a problem with the finance chief himself, Allen forced Delta into adopting more severe financial measures later on—in the process, perhaps, dooming himself in the eyes of the board."

Graphics used in the article included a timeline across the top of one page, showing key events in Delta's recent history, such as economic ups and downs, and executive changes. There was also an "instrument panel" of relevant financial data.

The authoritative development of the broader issues—about lessons in CFO-CEO relations, and in dealing with the board of directors—was made possible through interviews with other CFOs and outside management experts about Delta's experience. Most were delighted with the fresh example that the Allen-Roeck saga represented. They compared it with previous examples of executive disputes and board conflicts, and some described their own successes or failures in dealing with similar situations, leading to an instructive sidebar. Challenging the CEO in front of the board, said one former Apple Computer CFO who had done just that, was "like walking into a church and saying there was no God." It's "a painful process for an individual who doesn't have some thick skin."

Study #2
"Taming SAP"—Hard Questions About Software

While the Delta article started with the discovery of something the general media left out, the idea for *CFO's* March 1996 cover story, on problems with software from German software giant SAP AG, came right from the top: the magazine's editorial advisory board. Often, *CFO* uses its 12-member board of corporate-finance specialists to help editors troll for some tough issues that regular sources might be reluctant to discuss. In this case, the advisory board suggested targeting consultants—those outside experts hired to help companies deal with the complexities of business, but who often end up grating on their clients, while draining their checkbooks. Gradually, the board discussion focused on one particular group of consultants: those helping companies work with the popular R/3 client-server software made by SAP.

SAP's R/3 was designed to allow management of all major business processes in real time—what consultants call "enterprise resource planning," or ERP—and it had indeed broken new ground for CFOs by giving them unprecedented control. But while it was in many ways a dream product, its implementation was fraught with glitches. And given how expensive it was, R/3 had quietly started drawing some poor reviews. For *CFO,* it was left to confirm the extent of the discontent, and to crystallize the issue in an article aimed at unsuspecting finance chiefs.

After a few false starts—CFOs investing so heavily in the new, top-of-the-line software were embarrassed by its flaws—a few companies gradually stepped forward with their gripes. To others, any appearance of a "bandwagon" was enough to get them started; an avalanche of complaints followed. The main writer, technology editor John

Xenakis, who worked on a freelance basis, concentrated on the amazing things that R/3 could do. It was left to senior editor Edward Teach to elaborate on the problems, and the response of SAP. The trick of the story was to combine both elements in a way that would give readers a sense of R/3's promise, as well as its perils. It took dozens of interviews with R/3 users, consultants and others to paint an accurate picture.

After describing the dream—"to control all major business processes in real time, via a single software architecture, on a client-server computing platform"—the article then spelled out the dark side: "But reality, as more and more dreamers are discovering, can bite." Implementations are marked by "the dazzling complexity of the software and the dearth of consulting expertise" available to companies. At the same time, R/3 forces companies "to modify their business procedures to conform to SAP's strict integration requirements. That's a tall order, to put it mildly." One after another, company executives then ticked off their problems with the specific problems with the system.

Given its opportunity to reply to the criticism, SAP—a major *CFO* magazine advertiser—seemed surprised at the level of discontent that had been unearthed. And some at SAP worried that the negative comments from companies would hurt business. But one incident reported to the *CFO* editors suggested that others had observed the balance that the magazine worked so hard to maintain. An information executive whose company had just decided to buy R/3 got a marked-up copy of the article from his boss, with criticisms highlighted in yellow. The executive returned it to his boss with the positive parts highlighted—and the company went ahead with the implementation, better informed about the problems that lay ahead.

More than a year later, companies like Hershey Foods began reporting write-offs and operating problems related to their ERP software. Hershey, in fact, failed for the first time to capitalize on Halloween candy sales because of its ERP problems. And later still, *The Wall Street Journal* ran a story very similar to *CFO's* on the front page. It had taken the general-circulation business press that long to catch up with a significant information-technology trend that a trade magazine's editorial advisory board had spotted, and helped it develop.

"The SAP story was an important turning point for *CFO* magazine, because it demonstrated to the publisher and ad sales staff that a story critical of an advertiser could actually have a positive impact on ad sales," says editor Julia Homer. "SAP increased its advertising in *CFO* as a result, and the magazine gained more visibility and respect overall. The fact that our readers, SAP's customers, began asking SAP more questions as a result of our story did more to convince SAP of the importance of *CFO* magazine than any research could have."

Study # 3
"Where Finance Education Fails"—Giving Training a Grade

CFO's editors had made up their minds in 1997 to do a feature on university-based finance education, even before they had identified the precise issue. And they started with a readership survey to see what CFOs thought about the subject. The responses, by facsimile and by email helped spell out what became a compelling theme—that the academically popular move toward teaching theoretical and strategic finance was overshadowing instruction in the "basics" that corporate finance departments require of newly minted MBAs. Many graduates, the survey suggested, were often unprepared for entry-level finance jobs that involved dealing with routine areas like employee benefits or cash management. In short, they were being prepared to be CFOs, but not for the assistant-treasurer posts they were hired to occupy, and which were to give them their on-the-job business experience. Furthermore, the recent graduates often were weak in communications skills, seemed ill-prepared to deal with ethical challenges, and had a tough time adjusting to corporate cultures that prevailed at the companies where they landed.

Four main stories were designed, after a historical introduction describing the meteoric rise of the Master of Business Administration degree itself, with this writer in-house, and *CFO* freelance contributing editor Stephen Barr combining to split up much of the work. The first article, "Incomplete Education," explored our survey results, sampling widely divergent reactions from finance professors around the country. It featured thoughts from a number of survey participants who told us they were willing to be interviewed. Some said their companies were having to make up for shortcomings among the MBAs they hired by designing their own supplementary training programs for the nuts and bolts of finance, and concentrating on corporate culture and ethics.

Once the first story established that schools in general gave finance theory too much emphasis, and finance practice not enough, the second story ("Ethically Challenged") showed how unevenly ethics courses were designed. The third ("Off the Shelf . . . Off the Mark") looked at the world of executive education, examining why there are so few programs dedicated to useful finance topics. And the final installment ("A School of Their Own") presented cases of companies that had created their own finance training programs.

The 18-page treatment allowed *CFO* to offer two useful charts: one listing the top schools for finance, with details about each; the other presenting some of the more-interesting executive education programs in finance. Mainly, though, the articles were driven by the desire to give readers a chance to be heard about a problem that was close to their hearts, and to propose solutions. "There's no way that a hotshot out of [the University of] Chicago, or any other school, will be able to handle the complex nuances of dealing with the business world right away," one CFO, a Chicago graduate, told us. And the article did its best to explain why.

One interesting nuance the reporting turned up for Barr and me: universities seemed very willing to knock the approach of their competing schools. That gave us good leverage to go from school to school, examining strengths and weaknesses of individual programs—and presenting the universities' defense against what other schools said.

Every year since, *CFO* has revisited some element of the finance education problem. And our sources from the first article, along with new academics every year, have continued to help us track the progress in the field.

Study # 4

"The Corporate Connection"—Drug Money on the Bottom Line

Much as the Delta Airlines management dispute evolved into a story with broader implications, *CFO* in March 2001 turned straight news into an issue-based story examining how drug money can find its way into the coffers of unwitting companies—with serious repercussions.

The idea for the story, headlined "The Corporate Connection," originated with a *Frontline* Public Broadcasting Service telecast that was basically an overview of America's war on drugs. *CFO* senior writer Tim Reason noted a fleeting reference to money laundering that involved corporations, and a mention of how Clinton-administration Attorney General Janet Reno had met in secret with the CEOs of several large companies to discuss the problem.

Looking for news reports on this apparent corporate entanglement in the drug war, Reason found little except a thin *New York Times* piece. But that got him going; he put in a call to General Electric Co. and talked to its communications director about references to the company in the *Times* story. He confirmed that GE had attended such a meeting, and provided additional background information. The Web revealed a wealth of information on money laundering, of course, but the most promising were stories about the Colombian Black Market Peso Exchange, or BMPE—and especially a Treasury Department report *The National Money Laundering Strategy for 2000,* noting the contacts among industry leaders designed to combat the BMPE. Also on the Web: a Treasury brochure with tips for detecting BMPE-based laundering, and describing how it worked.

All this, along with an initial conversation about the cost of the money laundering compliance program to GE, was enough to get Reason's story idea enthusiastically approved at a *CFO* story meeting. Then, it was on to the creation of a source list, and to real reporting. Treasury was eager to spread the word to companies about its new program, and sent *CFO* stacks of information. Included was a reference to a case involving Bell Helicopter, a unit of Textron Corp. The nuts and bolts of the Bell case, which became the lead for the *CFO* story, were in federal court documents in Alabama. But Reason found motions that had been filed by about 15 companies, including Phillip Morris, Federal Mogul, and others that would ultimately refuse to comment.

Circumventing the natural reluctance of companies to talk about a drug-money-laundering case was a challenge eased by the presence of Textron's CFO on the *CFO* editorial advisory board. He appreciated the significance of the story—and the importance of getting companies to talk about the problem—and provided access to top-level Bell finance people. Reason found himself able to tell the story of how Bell felt maligned by the government, asked to deal with an issue beyond the corporation's ability to police it.

The government, of course, took a very different viewpoint. The Customs Service provided an officer willing to talk: a former director of financial investigations, who sat on the BMPE Working Group, and had been among the first to testify about the issue before Congress back in 1997. From agency officials, Reason got the counterpoint to Bell Helicopter's view.

One government contact wasn't a U.S. official at all, but an official at the Colombian customs agency, called DIAN. This proved one of his more difficult interviews, requiring several calls to Colombia, and straining Reason's Spanish vocabulary. Finally, though, the DIAN official provided a passionate quote about the terrorist bombings racking his country and their drug connections, and a plaintive plea for better cooperation from American corporations.

Other interview sources included "good corporate citizen" voices at GE and Whirlpool, who were happy to cooperate. Among corporations like Federal-Mogul and Phillip Morris, who had also been caught in the case that also tripped up Bell Helicopters, official comments were thinner. But other sources emerged—including a former IRS attorney relocated at accounting firm Ernst & Young, and a former assistant U.S. attorney in private practice helping companies deal with the money laundering issue—and *CFO* had the big picture.

"The traffic in illegal drugs is a global problem, and money-laundering schemes take many forms," the article said. "But for American companies like Fort Worth-based Bell, the Colombian Black Market Peso Exchange poses by far the greatest risk. Described by former U.S. Customs commissioner Raymond W. Kelly as 'perhaps the largest, most insidious money-laundering system in the Western Hemisphere,' the BMPE enables drug traffickers to use their profits to buy consumer goods in the States, masking the money's illicit origins. For U.S. companies, that's a problem that goes far beyond the public relations nightmare of having their products connected with the narcotics trade, because it is a crime to knowingly accept money that is connected to drug trafficking."

The article got noticed by others in the business media—and won a Silver ASBPE award—but senior writer Reason remembers it most because of the thrill of the chase it involved. "It was an all-consuming experience for almost a solid month, where lead led to lead, and each new court document sparked searches for other court documents," he says. "The story still ranks as among the most exciting I have done, not because of the sexy subject matter, but because of the way the picture and the story came together."

Study # 5

"The Fear of All Sums"—An Era of Corporate Scandals and Reforms

When the complex network of illegal accounting practices at Enron Corp. unraveled starting in 2001—the first of many finance-department abuses involving such one-time high-fliers as WorldCom and Tyco International—the first reaction at *CFO* was intense embarrassment. The same intricate financial engineering that masked their abuses, it turned out, had been celebrated in the pages of *CFO* in the late 1990s. "It was our darkest hour," says editor Julia Homer, who quickly eliminated the "Excellence in Finance" awards program, judged by independent finance experts, that had given *CFO's* blessing on executives who had since been discredited. (NOTE TO EDITORS: Beware of naming even your industry stars as "executives of the year.")

Soon, though, the staff began to redouble its efforts to get to the bottom of the scandals. In addition to being the big corporate-finance issue of the era—and one the magazine was in a unique position to explain—the staff knew that it owed it to our readership.

"At an off-site meeting at my home," says Homer, "we planned a four-part series on the different dimensions of corporate fraud." Of course, the series evolved as 2002 progressed and new scandals unfolded, along with initial proposals for reform. But what the staff cobbled together in a day of brainstorming there in her family room in rural Hopkinton, Massachusetts—after breaking down the problem into its major elements—was remarkably prescient. And the approach was at odds with what most of the finance community was saying. "The official reaction from financial associations at the time was 'it's just a few bad apples,' but we decided not to pander to our audience by agreeing with that view," according to the editor. "We incorporated reader opinions on specific issues through four surveys." But in the end, digging deeper, *CFO's* conclusion was that "the problems were systemic, not individual," she says. "We didn't shrink from addressing the way conflicts of interests and greed had resulted in bad business decisions."

The August cover story, headlined "The Fear of All Sums," kicked off the four-partner with an examination of such abused corporate techniques as Enron's "special purpose entities," and discussed how the disclosure and other remedies being made by companies on their own were often inadequate, and even meaningless. September's "No More Mr. Nice Guy" concentrated on how one major corporate accounting "watchdog," the system of outside auditors, had instead become a lapdog. The story showed why this important corporate control element was in dire need of an overhaul. Another problem—how boards of directors had become too lax in their role—was featured in the cover story "Board Games." But the culmination of the series was without doubt "Now What?" the October theme issue that examined why the scandals happened, and why it would be difficult for proposed reforms to fix things.

In focusing repeatedly on the problems within corporate finance, *CFO* put to the test its practice of giving advertisers the opportunity to respond to adverse comment, or to pull its ads from a particular issue. That's because "so many of our advertisers, not to mention our readers, have been criticized for their roles in financial scandals," says Homer. The Magazine of the Year honor thus was especially valued by *CFO*. In addition, its feature series and the October issue won Gold awards from ASBPE, among the record of 10 national awards the organization presented to the magazine.

Increasingly, all the attention given to the finance-department fiascos and the calls for reform has turned *CFO* itself into a respected news source—cited by other publications as they prepare their own issue-based stories to try to explain the complexities of the situation. It is an enviable position for a magazine to be in, especially after that

Publication Launch

<big><big>2</big></big>

Think Like a Publisher, Create Like an Editor

⌐Conard Holton

Few endeavors in publishing are more rewarding—personally and professionally—than starting a new publication. Fair warning, however: the effort involved can be all-consuming; the frustrations are many; and the odds of success are long. But don't miss the opportunity.

Most trade publishing companies are genuinely interested in launching new publications. They understand that it's important to the vitality and growth of the company, and they know it's a risky venture that may not succeed. They do it because one successful new magazine will more than pay for many failures and could provide the company with substantial long-term growth.

As an editor, you may have any or all of these reasons for starting a new magazine:

- *Entrepreneurial impulse.* You see an opportunity that no one else has taken advantage of or done in a uniquely effective way. As a result, you can create something that is familiar to readers, but adds new value. Or perhaps you can take an entirely new approach. The satisfaction comes from finding this approach, bringing it to print, and then keeping it fresh and ahead of the competition.

- *Financial betterment.* Certainly the goal of a publishing company is to make a profit, and you must be able to evaluate carefully the potential of a new profit center. You enhance your career prospects if you are creative and able to deliver new products, even if you are not completely successful. However, given the risk that companies assume by investing in a start-up and the time lag before profits are made, immediate reward should not be your motive. In fact, if it is your primary motive, seek a career in sales rather than editorial.

- *Staff development.* One of the best ways to motivate people is to give them new challenges and opportunities. The rewards of being part of a start-up

Conard Holton is executive editor of Laser Focus World *and editor-in-chief of* WDM Solutions. *Holton has been a technical editor for 20 years and wrote a history of the cleanup of Three Mile Island after the nuclear accident.*

publication include intense education and experience, stimulating conversations, hair-raising deadlines, and the kind of camaraderie that can be hard to
find in established publications. If the start-up is successful, new career paths
are opened. If it is not, failure brings important experience and visibility
within your company and the publishing industry.

- *Market positioning.* Although an industry may not be mature enough to support a profitable magazine, starting a new publication for the industry may be
  a good strategic move. Getting into a market; establishing industry relationships, an advertising presence, and a reader base; and helping to define how
  an industry communicates are all excellent foundations for future returns.
  Convincing a publishing company to invest in unproven markets is a challenging proposition, but can prove worth the effort and risk.

For an editor, two paths to a new publication exist, each with its own advantages
and disadvantages:

- *Formal start-up.* Publishing organizations generally set aside or can find funds
  for new ventures, whether launching new magazines or services, or acquiring
  new franchises. Getting a new magazine funded from this source usually requires a detailed business plan and selling the concept up the organizational
  hierarchy to the highest decision-maker, often a company president or board
  of directors. The advantage of this route is full organizational support for the
  project, along with a commitment of resources from all departments, ade-
  quate marketing and staff, and enough financial backing to carry through a
  few years of losses. The disadvantage may be less flexibility and more internal company reporting requirements.
- *Guerrilla start-up.* By leveraging existing staff and budgets, it may be possible
  to position a new publication so that it gains market visibility and acceptance
  without formal approval or additional investment. One way to do this is to
  start a supplement to an existing publication. It's a difficult path since it relies
  on cooperation from other departments, little marketing, and extra work from
  current staff. But the risks are lower and potential for success is good since
  there is little additional investment in resources and a supplement can be
  grown as market conditions dictate. Depending on the size of the parent
  company, such a publication should face less oversight and have more
  flexibility. It also may not need a formal business plan.

To launch a new trade publication, an editor must think like a publisher—analyzing several obvious but perhaps unfamiliar parameters over which you may not have
much control. Here are some questions to ask yourself:

1. Economic climate
   - Is the general economy strong or weak? What is the trend? Where are the
     hot spots and how are they related to macro conditions?
   - What's the global picture? Does it correspond to markets in the United States?

2. Market opportunity
   - What's the competitive landscape: what magazines, Web sites, newsletters, or other media cover the market, and how?
   - Who is not being served? Can they be clearly identified or are they part of evolving markets?
   - Do companies or organizations have money that could be spent on advertising new products or helping them expand into new fields? Are advertising budgets fixed once a year or is there discretionary money available during the year?
   - What are the sources of revenue or funding in this market: consumers, other industries, government agencies, universities, venture capitalists, investment bankers? What interests them?

3. Corporate culture
   - Does your publishing company encourage risk taking? Does it prefer to start new ventures, strengthen existing products, or acquire new products?
   - What sort of resources does your company provide to new ventures? Do these ventures get special funding or must the resources come from existing budgets and staff?
   - If your target market is in flux, as most businesses are, is your company willing to invest the time, energy, and money in a project that may have, at best, only a limited successful life?

4. Personal commitment
   - Since startups involve many unknowns and considerable risk, how much do you trust your own judgment? Do you have or need a mentor or sponsor in management?
   - In evaluating the prospects for a new venture, how analytical are you? In other words, have you done enough research to be confident of the logic, yet are you willing to rely on intuitive feelings to motivate and inspire?
   - Are you ready for the personal commitment, concentration, and drive it takes to make a new venture successful?
   - Is there a formal reward policy? Does it depend on success? Does it matter? (See reasons to start a magazine.)
   - How well do you handle failure, especially if it happens over considerable time?

How you answer these questions will vary, but the questions reflect the inevitable challenges of starting a new venture in publishing. They should be the subjects covered in your business plan.

A Case Study—WDM Solutions

We launched *WDM Solutions* in September 1999 as a supplement to one of Penn Well's most established and successful magazines, *Laser Focus World,* which has been covering optoelectronics technology and applications for more than 35 years. Optoelectronics—also known as photonics—is the technology of manipulating light. It

Evolution of an idea. As it moved from a magazine supplement to a magazine in its own right, *WDM Solutions* built on its identity as an authority on the use of laser optics in telecommunications.

includes such familiar applications as lasers for DVD players, optics in telescopes, and CCD devices in digital cameras. Most of the magazine coverage, however, is aimed at technical people involved in research, product development, or industry.

One area of *Laser Focus World's* coverage began to take off in the late 1990s: optical fiber and related equipment used in telecommunications networks. The growing telecom "bubble" was related to the dot-com bubble, and was based on the belief that the telecommunications industry needed to build tremendous new infrastructure to handle the real and hoped-for growth of the Internet. In the United States, the deregulation of the industry in 1996 spawned hundreds of new providers of telecommunications services to compete with the likes of AT&T and Verizon, and several thousand new companies hoping to make equipment for the industry. Visits to tradeshows, review of market studies and Wall Street reports, and discussion with advertisers convinced us that there was an opportunity for a new magazine in the field.

WDM Solutions was conceived as a supplement, and later became an independent magazine. Its mission is to provide engineers with design and technical information about wavelength-division multiplexing (WDM) technology. Simply put, WDM is a technology that greatly increases the capacity, speed, and potential of telecommunications.

The first supplement of *WDM Solutions* was a 44-page portfolio that attracted significant advertising, and was considered an excellent start. Two years later, as an independent magazine, it was a 180-page folio, with very strong advertising. Two and a half years after that, the advertising had essentially vanished and *WDM Solutions* returned to the status of a supplement. The telecommunications industry had overbuilt the infrastructure and so the market collapsed with breathtaking speed.

In the course of those four and a half years, the magazine evolved from a few basic tutorial engineering articles to sophisticated coverage of an evolving industry, with articles on new research, interviews with technical leaders, market analysis, and opinion pieces. It also faced all the major issues that confront a new publication.

WDM Solutions is an anomaly in magazine publishing in the sense that such rapid growth in a startup is rare. Successful startups are more likely to show a general upward trend in readership and advertising sales, with some slower or faster periods. Yet the story of *WDM Solutions* highlights the key issues that must be addressed by any startup, and reflects the market cycles that will always be with us and impact whatever ventures we pursue.

Audience—Readers and Advertisers

We aimed to cover technical content that concerned engineers, designers, and engineering managers—and the advertisers who wanted to reach them. Other readers, including executive management and investors, subscribed, but the editorial content assumed that the reader had a fundamental grasp of the technology. At the peak, there were 35,000 BPA-qualified subscribers to *WDM Solutions.*

Strengths: By targeting a relatively small but critical audience, the magazine could establish credibility with the people who actually tested and recommended products for purchase. Magazines with broader coverage could not provide such technical depth for working engineers. There was a great hunger for technical information because the industry was relatively young, the technology was new and difficult, and many engineers from other industries were joining the booming market sector. The result was a magazine that was positioned to reach a critical buying audience.

Weaknesses: By focusing in such depth on a specific technology, *WDM,* the magazine, was vulnerable to market trends or technologies. When the bubble burst, the readers and advertisers that remained shifted focus to other technologies and survival strategies. General business and technology magazines covering the industry had flexibility and could provide business coverage, which became more important to readers than technology during the downturn (not to mention the fact that in telecom, hundreds of companies and their marketing budgets vanished in a matter of months).

Competitive Landscape

Although numerous magazines covered telecommunications, most focused on broad issues such as regulatory policy or concerns of the service providers such as AT&T or Verizon. In fact, when *WDM Solutions* was founded, the number of magazines focused on telecommunications from the perspective of equipment makers was limited to three main competitors.

Strengths: By focusing on a narrow, technical niche, we had a stronger (if more limited) position with engineers than any of our competitors.

Weaknesses: Although the focus of each magazine was slightly different, the advertising base for all four was the same. The result was that we competed fiercely for sales. Fortunately the market was large enough to support the competition, and *WDM Solutions* emerged as a strong contender for the second largest portion of market share.

Editorial Content and Staff

Since we started the magazine as a supplement—in a sense keeping it under the radar—most support staff was shared with other magazines. The editorial content was premised on contributed technical articles from the industry, with a few interviews or research notes added by contributing editors. By using contributed articles, the editorial staff could be kept quite small and focused on editing rather than writing. Thus we never had more than a chief editor and one senior editor, and relied on *Laser Focus World* to provide services such as managing editor.

For content, we decided not to cover business news, since that was well covered by other media and several Web sites devoted to the industry. Instead, we focused on technical content, but provided several different sections that allowed multiple points of entry for a reader. The basic sections were: 1) an editor's desk; 2) short research notes from laboratories; 3) columns such as interviews with technology experts, market analysis of technical trends, and opinion pieces; 4) technical features; and 5) tutorial articles written by contributing editors.

Strengths: With our premise that really useful technical articles could best be written by engineers, we put our energy into rigorous soliciting and editing. This approach required that the editors have a very good understanding of the technology, rather than being generalists. We understood that contributors would be representing their company and its products and philosophy, but we found that with coaching, they were quite willing to write articles that were fairly objective and not overtly commercial.

Overall, our insistence on non-commercial presentations worked since from the beginning no reader—or author—saw company names or products in the articles, and most realized that their own credibility, along with that of their company, depended on maintaining the standard. The fact that the industry was growing very fast and was highly competitive meant that we could be selective and demanding of our contributors.

Weaknesses: Because we had a small staff that was not oriented toward news, and because we relied on contributed articles, we could not always control the content or market coverage with as much timeliness or focus as we could have if we had a dedicated writing staff. Finding qualified technical editors or contributing writers was also a continuing challenge.

When the market turned down, the number of companies dropped, and the staff of those surviving companies were under great pressure to promote their products without objectivity. So it became more difficult to maintain our editorial standards. Ironically, as the revenue of companies in the industry shrank, many of them focused more on marketing tactics such as contributing articles and visiting editorial offices rather than spending money on advertising. We were not the only magazine to see the number of proposed articles rise in direct proportion to the decline in advertising and, hence, the space available to publish the articles.

Graphics and Design

When we began, we had the advantage of a strong market and so were able to use the best paper, finish, and graphics. We gave our graphic artist and art director lots of leeway since (a) they were very creative people who are usually constrained within strict formats and dense technical subject matter; and (b) we wanted a new look that combined playfulness, high brand recognition, and solid technical information.

Strengths: Most technology, especially telecommunications, is visually uninteresting, since most equipment consists of boxes or stacks of boxes connected by wires. We managed to get a few good photos from authors, and we produced great technical line drawings to illustrate the articles, but we also made sure to include pictures of people whenever possible and to keep the design clean and open. Most importantly, at each monthly cover meeting our staff debated with energy what kind of non-technical image could convey the cover story. The resulting cover art, which was reused throughout the magazine and for marketing, was a motivator for us all.

Weaknesses: The use of a graphic artist is more expensive and demanding than using vendor photos of technology and embellishing them, or relying on stock images.

Circulation

The most surprising—and potentially difficult—aspect of publishing for an editor to learn is the crucial role of circulation, and how it is managed. Beginning as a supplement to *Laser Focus World* enabled us to reach an audited subscriber base of 70,000 engineers and designers, with approximately 15,000 overseas subscribers. That is a relatively large number among high-tech trade publications, and commands a premium for advertising rates. Of that number, we estimated perhaps half were specifically involved in telecommunications or were considering it. The BPA statement identified many of these subscribers, but it was not designed to clearly identify all of them within a complex optoelectronics market.

Strengths: When we launched *WDM Solutions* as an independent magazine in September 2001, we set the circulation goal at 35,000, meaning we had to find 35,000 people who would fill out a paper or Web-based form to meet BPA requirements within 12 months. We actually reached that number in nine months, a very fast sign-up rate in our business. Of that number, 5,000 subscribers came from Europe and 5,000 from Asia, primarily Japan and China. We could keep the price of the ads relatively high because the industry was flush with venture capital money and competition.

Weaknesses: When the market broke, 35,000 subscribers was far too many. Not only was the number of employed engineers falling, but the cost of building and maintaining that size circulation was out of proportion to the new advertising revenue stream. Over the course of two years, we continually cut the size of our subscriber base, which caused difficulties with justifying other overhead costs and the price of ads.

The lesson for an editor is a difficult one: We naturally want to reach as many readers as we can, and as many as the market will bear. But the smart publishing strategy restricts the circulation to a number that balances reader demand, production and distribution costs, advertising revenue, and market trends. A small, well-positioned niche magazine can be very successful both financially and editorially.

Sales Team

The sales staff and sales strategies are usually far from an editor's domain, yet if you're involved in a start-up publication, you need to consider the strategic sales plan and projected revenue. You also need to work closely with the sales force to identify potential advertisers and explain the mission and editorial calendar. An enthusiastic editor can motivate the sales team into making a startup successful. Because *WDM Solutions* was a spinoff of *Laser Focus World,* the same sales team sold both magazines.

Strengths: From traditional Laser Focus World advertisers, sales were excellent. With two related publications to sell, the sales team could create very appealing packages for advertisers. The booming nature of the telecom market meant advertisers were seeking marketing avenues in magazines like *WDM Solutions.*

Weaknesses: The sales team was unfamiliar with and had difficulty developing new advertisers from related but distant markets. Also, with multiple magazines to sell, the focus of the sales team was diluted. A sales team dedicated to a single publication probably works best in the long term, and if this publication had sufficient market support, it would have been necessary to move in this direction.

Franchise Opportunities

If there is a real opportunity to create a new magazine, chances are there are also opportunities for related products such as tradeshows, seminars, Web sites, newsletters, and a buyers' guide. At *WDM Solutions,* we ran two technical seminars, had a Web site and e-newsletter, and published a buyers' guide in conjunction with *Laser Focus World.*

Strengths: Expanding the franchise is a time-honored method of adding revenue and increasing brand recognition. We created a one-day technical seminar that was initially very successful. A forum in Tokyo co-sponsored with the Japanese magazine *Nikkei Electronics* help spread the brand in Japan. The Web site was popular because the complete archives of the magazine were available, and many engineers from around the world used the information.

Weaknesses: Like any stretching of resources, these activities risk diluting the focus on the main product, the magazine, and siphoning off time and staff to less profitable activities. The Web, as every editor knows, is insatiable and the return in terms of advertising revenue never stimulated significant investment for us to create unique content. Since we were not focused on business news, the technical archives had much greater value to our visitors.

Parting Shots

If you have the opportunity to help start a new magazine, be prepared to own it—for better or for worse. It easily becomes (and should become) a very personal mission. Just keep in mind that it's still a business. It has to justify its existence in the economic sense of the word, along with justifying the act of reading it. So remember, think like a publisher, create like an editor.

See chapter exercise at the back of this book.

Editorial Direction

3

The Well-Defined Redesign

Stacey Moncrieff and Pamela Geurds Kabati

Trade publications are among the most visible reflections of the industry they serve—both to their readers and to the public. But knowing that their primary purpose is service journalism, their editors can underestimate the importance of the image they convey. In combination with relevant editorial, good design can often mean the difference between whether your product will sink or swim.

Making the Redesign Decision

Any business magazine that's been in publication for more than a few months is bound to run into design conflicts:

- There's never enough space to run the kind of art/topics/expert voices you want to use;
- The reader benefit of your articles isn't made clear in the design;
- Your type/art/look is dated;
- You don't have a consistent way to accommodate recurring elements, such as online references.

Whatever your beefs, at some point you'll be ready to move from complaints (or constant tweaks) to a full-blown redesign. How do you know when it's time? Some signs:

1. *You're planning a major change in your editorial.* Say you've been publishing 5,000-word feature articles, but readership research suggests you should add more expert columns and shift to shorter features with more entry points. You'll need a design that fits the new content your editors will be producing. Likewise, if there have been big changes in the industry you cover and your editorial mix hasn't kept pace, it may be time for an editorial restructuring and redesign.
2. *Your magazine's design is at odds with your readership.* Your design needs to not only package the editorial content but also telegraph the right tone. Are you throwing avant garde design at a traditional audience? Business

---

Stacey Moncrieff is editor of Realtor® Magazine, *published by the National Association of Realtors®. Pamela Geurds Kabati is vice president of publications and editorial director at the National Association of Realtors®.*

magazines are often mailed directly to readers' businesses. *Ask:* Would our readers be proud to have their customers and colleagues see "their" magazine? Answering that question requires an intimate understanding of your readers. Consult your own readership research and other research you can find about members of your industry. (Trade associations are good sources of this information.) Get your editors together to talk about their interactions with industry members at trade shows and in the development of stories. Develop a "picture" of your readers and ask yourself whether your design fits that picture.

3. *Every month you're struggling to make things "work."* Consider an overhaul if you're regularly struggling to fit in your core package of editorial or you're coming up with great editorial or design ideas that just don't have a home in your current format.

4. *You haven't redesigned in five years or more.* It's not unusual today for consumer magazines to have frequent facelifts—even every two or three years. After that amount of time your typefaces and artwork will likely appear dated. If a president of the United States has come and gone since your last redesign, it's time to consider a change.

5. *Reader responsiveness is low.* Business magazines center on their readers' livelihoods and should regularly hit readers' hot buttons with regard to the industry they serve. If your readership displays a noted lack of responsiveness, you may not be giving them the content they want. Before you make any change to the editorial package or design, however, you'll want to proactively seek readers' input through surveys or focus groups.

Anatomy of a Redesign

Planning Basics

Once you've determined that a redesign is in your future, put together a plan of action. Consider your timeline, budget, and who needs to be involved in the decision-making.

Timeline

As a general rule, leave about 18 months to complete all the steps in the redesign process. You may have a certain date you want to launch your redesign—the first issue of the year or the issue that coincides with your industry's biggest trade show. If so, you'll need to work backward from that date and fit the redesign into your available time. Some magazines with the luxury of plenty of editorial and design support have completed redesigns in as little as 10 months. Depending on the depth of the redesign, it can be done in as little as two months. For a 2002 redesign of *Realtor® Magazine,* we planned for the full 18 months and timed our redesign to launch during a large real estate industry annual conference sponsored by our publisher, the National Association of Realtors®.

Budget

It's important to know what your available resources are before you embark on a redesign. Talk with your publisher upfront and agree on a bottom-line number. Be sure to include the cost of:

- *Readership research*. If you don't have up-to-date information on the readers or potential readers of your magazine, get some. A full-scale study conducted by mail typically costs $35,000 to $40,000—but you often can get a good picture of your audience for much less with a combination of online surveying (if you have or can acquire a good e-mail list of people in your industry), focus groups with readers or potential readers, and business intelligence reports developed by your editors from their attendance at industry conferences and trade shows.
- *Outside design services*. Your designer(s) will need to continue producing the book throughout the redesign and likely won't have time for both jobs. Also an outside design consultant can bring a fresh perspective to your magazine, helping you work through design dilemmas that have been plaguing the magazine. It's difficult to come up with rule-of-thumb costs for outside design services, but it's not unusual to pay $40,000–$50,000 plus travel expenses.
- *Design explorations*. You'll go through a lot of paper and printing in pursuit of the winning design. As you refine page designs, consider investing in royalty-free stock art to place on the mock pages. The use of actual text and art makes it easier for you to hone your redesign and give your publisher and staff a clearer understanding of what you're aiming for.
- *Typefaces/font families*. If you plan to explore typefaces that aren't part of your existing font library, you'll need to purchase the new font family or families from the type house or foundry that owns them. Costs can vary, so be sure to identify a price range and incorporate the expense into your plan.
- *Promotion to readers and advertisers*. You'll need to let your advertisers and readers know the new design is coming. Your promotion can be as simple as letters to advertisers and house ads in the magazine, or as elaborate as creation of a prototype magazine with real copy and art. Plan your promotion budget accordingly.

Decision-Making Chain

Determine upfront who's directing your redesign. Remember: Design is in service of your editorial. Therefore, generally the editor, not the art director, should be in charge of a redesign. However, a successful redesign requires respect for the art director's vision and teamwork. You can't have a successful redesign unless the editor and art director are both clear on the goals and collaborate closely every step of the way.

Also, identify who needs to be involved along the way and how and when you want to communicate with the ultimate decision-makers, typically, the editorial director

REALTOR® Magazine REDESIGN—Timeline

DATE	PHASE I CONTENT & GOAL ESTABLISHMENT	PHASE II DESIGN DEVELOPMENT	PHASE III IMPLEMENTATION
10/1	Cover mocks completed		
9/28–10/25	Roundtables completed		
11/2	Roundtable reports compiled; observations synthesized for ed. staff, management; Review consultant proposals		
11/6	Review reports, team redesign plans outline project scope; Interview consultants (PGK, SAM, JF)	Consultant input	
11/12	Mission and vision for both editorial and graphic—special Monday meeting	Development of nameplate and structural headings begins	
11/19	Core editorial developed—special Monday meeting		
11/21	Mission, vision and core editorial recommendations to PGK	Structural prototype built—thumbnails and electronic files	
11/28	Revisions: mission, vision and core editorial		
11/29	Mission, vision and core editorial recommendations presented to FS—special meeting		
12/5	Revisions to mission, vision and core editorial	Translate mission, vision and core editorial into visual language	
12/10	Organization of core elements	Design production begins Treatment decisions: –Nameplate development cont. –Overall look: Structure, dept., column and feature banners –Headline fonts and sizes –Body fonts and sizes –Departments, Columns, Features –Misc. elements: bullets, end notes, jumps, initial caps, lists, source lines. REALTOR® trademarked terms, designations, references (to magazine, website, and other NAR websites).	

REALTOR® Magazine REDESIGN—Timeline (cont.)

DATE	PHASE I CONTENT & GOAL ESTABLISHMENT	PHASE II DESIGN DEVELOPMENT	PHASE III IMPLEMENTATION
1/14		Midpoint review with consultant (JF, PGK, SAM, and maybe FS)	Consider how to promote
2/4		Design mocks (three treatments) to SAM, PGK	
2/4–2/15		Revisions	
2/19		Design mocks _with recommendation_ to FS—special meeting	Electronic template created for monthly production
2/25		Design direction established	
2/25–3/14		Design refinement	Prototype created for ad staff
3/15		Refined design presented to FS—special meeting	
3/18		Design refinements to Reds, Pubs-Web staff—special Monday meeting	
3/19–3/29		Revisions	Prototype for ad staff final (29)
3/29–5/7		Outstanding design decisions resolved	Spec book drafted
5/15			FINAL DESIGN W/SPECS
5/31			Design of Sept 02 issue begins

From National Association of Realtors®. Reprinted by permission of editor.

and/or the publisher (*see "Keeping Decision-Makers in the Loop" below*). You don't want a redesign by committee, but it's important to ensure that your staff has a voice in your redesign. As you go through the redesign process we've outlined below, you'll see points at which we recommend bringing editors and writers—and sometimes advertising and marketing staff—into the process.

Taking Action

Once you've laid out your plan, it's time to act. We recommend following these eight steps:

Step 1: *Create a "picture" of your readers.* Assuming you have the research you need, bring your editors together, and review the main points of the research. *Ask:* What is the essence of the work our readers perform? How is their business changing?

What skills and tools do they need to be successful in their business today? What adjectives would you use to describe our readers? What adjectives would you *not* use to describe our readers?

Develop the brainstorming notes into a draft document and share it with all the editors. Give editors the opportunity to suggest refinements.

Step 2: *Write an editorial mission statement, or review your existing mission.*   For a business magazine, writing a mission statement is a straightforward task: Your mission is to help members of the industry you serve achieve success in their business. Still, put some time into your statement. Get your editors together to review your current statement alongside the picture of your readers. *Ask:* Does this statement capture what we do and what our members need? Is it succinct and memorable? Does it clearly differentiate us from our competitors?

Draft a refined mission statement and share it with all the editors. Give editors the opportunity to suggest refinements. Also, allow time for your design, advertising, and marketing staff to review the statement and give input.

Step 3: *Write a redesign brief.*   The brief is the formal statement of your redesign objectives. It answers the question: What do we want this redesign to accomplish? The brief outlines the design and editorial philosophy you want to apply, and it describes the kind of publication you want to be, using specific adjectives and phrases. For example, "Our magazine provides how-to information that our readers can act on immediately to achieve greater success in their business. We package articles in a way that makes it easy for readers to scan the main points, and we direct readers to additional online sources of information. We're also the eyes and ears of our readers, scanning the marketplace for trends that may affect their business. Our editorial and design tone is professional and modern, reflecting our young, upwardly mobile readers."

This brief is important, because it gets all parties off on a strong and clear direction. Your brief, like your mission statement, will be a touchstone for you throughout the redesign process, helping to guide decisions on your overall content mix, editorial structure, typefaces, color palette and logo treatment.

Typical subheads for a brief:

- *Executive Summary*—Outline who you are in relation to the industry you serve (e.g.: "We publish the essential business tool for 80,000 security professionals with pass-along readership of an additional 80,000, making ours the second-highest circulation magazine in the industry.") and what you hope to achieve with the redesign ("The magazine underwent a redesign four years ago. With this effort, we plan to solidify our brand and move it into the No. 1 slot in the crowded security category.")
- *General Objectives*—Outline areas for improvement in your design, as well as aspects of your current design that work and that you might like to carry forward or adapt in the new look.
- *Reader*—Spell out the picture of your reader that you created in Step 1.

- *Competition*—Business publications face competition both within their industry (*PC World* vs. *PC Week*) and with newsstand business magazines, such as *Forbes* and *Fortune*. Write an analysis of where you stand in relation to the competition. This analysis should support the "territory" you've staked in your mission statement and help your designer find important areas of emphasis in the redesign.
- *Logo*—The logo is the first step in branding your publication and telegraphing your editorial tone. Discuss what you want the new logo to achieve and what, if anything, is lacking in your existing logo.
- *Cover*—For the brief, talk about what has been successful and what hasn't been successful with your existing cover look. It's also important to spell out what you like to change and what text or design elements you want to keep when you redesign. You'll spell out a philosophy for the cover design later in the process.
- *Inside Pages*—Your new look needs to stand up to the "gutter test." That is, if your subscribers were to see a page of your magazine in the gutter (that is, torn from the context of your magazine) they'd recognize it immediately as your publication.
- *Trim Size*—Will it change or stay the same?

Your brief should also include your mission statement, the timeline and budget you developed, and any special advertising concerns, such as sizes and special positions that need to be considered. Make sure your publisher and editorial director are involved in the document and give their creative sign-off before you proceed to Step 4. Also, share the brief with your editors, designers, and advertising staff, and allow time for them to comment and provide input.

Step 4: *Develop your core editorial.* From the preparatory work you've done in Steps 1–3, development of your core editorial—that is, the regular columns and departments in your book—should flow naturally. Start by looking at the editorial you're currently producing. *Ask:* Does it fit the picture you've created of your readers? Does it achieve your mission? Then, look back at the readership research and pinpoint the topics most in demand by your readers. Simply providing more coverage of those topics in your redesigned book will increase your readers' satisfaction, according to Bill Billick, president of Media Research Corp. of America, Hellertown, Pa. Finally, scan your environment: Look at the hot-button issues that draw letters to the editor, the topics that get the most play in industry e-mail discussion groups, and the sessions that draw the most attendance at trade show education sessions.

Bring all that input to an editorial meeting, and have the editors brainstorm broad topic areas that your magazine should be covering on a regular basis. At *Realtor*® *Magazine,* for example, we determined that we needed to cover legal topics and sales techniques in every issue, but that other topics, such as commercial-investment real estate, could be covered less often.

Take the results of that meeting, and draft a core editorial document in the form of a chart. The document should break down, as specifically as possible, all of the content you propose to put in the redesigned book. If you want the opening department of your book to always include a news story, a trend story, a chart that tracks your industry, and a Washington update page, include those in the core. Make sure your core editorial conforms to a realistic page count for your magazine. Promising elements you don't have space to deliver will reduce your credibility both internally and with your readers.

Organize the chart as you envision the pieces flowing in the book—starting with the cover and working your way through to the back-page feature. The order of elements will likely change somewhat as you get further along in your redesign, but having at least a tentative order will help your designer create proper pacing in the book.

What's pacing? It's how a magazine flows from front to back. All well-designed books, like all good meals, have a beginning, middle, and end, says New York designer Ina Saltz. Your book's opening pages are like your place setting. Your front section is the appetizer and leads people into the meat—an editorial well that should be mostly uninterrupted by ads. From there, you should move to the salad course—a section of columns that present slightly lighter fare—followed on the inside back page by the dessert.

Make each entry in your core editorial chart as detailed as possible: Show the name of the column or department you're proposing, the length by page count or word count, a description, the art approach, and who on your staff will be responsible for the content. We also recommend including an entry for "feature well" in the chart with an estimate or a range of pages. Although your feature topics will change from month to month, having all your editorial in the chart will make it a useful tool for discussing editorial page counts and ad-edit ratios with your publisher.

Your full editorial and design staff should have time to review the core editorial. Make sure it's clear who's responsible for each element in the magazine, and give the staff an opportunity to comment and help you refine the elements.

Step 5: *Develop a design foundation.*   While you're refining the core editorial, begin designing the foundational elements of your book. Those elements include the logo, the cover philosophy, headline and body fonts, and color palette.

Logo

Your logo is your identity, your brand, your face. Your main consideration should be how it appears on the magazine cover. However, you should also consider how it'll reproduce on your media kit, stationery, business cards, and other identity material you create, such as t-shirts and coffee mugs.

The name of the game in choosing a logo is exploration. Try a lot of different typefaces and sizes. The font you choose should send the right message to your readers. *Builder* magazine (published by Hanley-Wood, Washington, D.C.), for homebuilders, has a strong, bold logo that conveys the image of solid construction. For *Realtor*® *Magazine,* which is aimed at people who sell and manage real estate, we wanted a typeface with a lighter touch, more finesse, more style. To find the right font for our 2002 redesign, we looked at consumer and business magazines we admired—particularly magazines whose demographics were close to those of our readers (median age of 51, high median household income, self-employed). We not only looked at font choices, we analyzed the size of logos in proportion to magazines' trim size. We determined that an appropriate size for us would be about one-fifth of the cover—big enough to have a presence without taking up too much of our 8-inch by 10-1/2 inch image space. After you select a font and size, consider refinements. Softening serifs or adding some other distinguishing mark can ensure that your logotype is uniquely your own.

Headline and Body Fonts

Finding the right headline and body fonts, like finding the right logo, is a matter of research. Set sample copy in different fonts. The variations are sometimes subtle but can make a big difference in readability and tone.

For body copy, be sure to try different type sizes with different leading options to see how readability is impacted. At *Realtor*® *Magazine,* we previously used 10.5-point body copy, which was easy on the eyes of our readers (median age: 51). With the re-design, we adopted 9.5-point type but kept the leading at 12. The result: Improved readability.

Ultimately, you want to limit your selection to two fonts—a serif and a sans serif face. For our redesign, we selected Miller as our serif and Benton as our sans serif. We use Miller for both headline and body copy. Benton is an accent face that we use for our logo as well as in some headlines, some sidebars, some callouts, and charts.

Both Miller and Benton are "full families" of type, meaning each offers us a wide range of variations—bold, extrabold, italic, condensed, and so on. This allows the designer an ample toolbox of fonts to create subtle changes in emphasis and focus. However, be careful how freely you use such choices; too much variety will water down your design. Rule of thumb: Standing elements should receive a consistent treatment; features can be more broadly defined. To aid in consistent font and style use, create style sheets in whatever page layout program you use to produce pages to ensure that your headline and body copy for core pages remained consistent. We al-low more variation in features.

Cover Philosophy

Creating compelling covers is probably the most challenging aspect of magazine production. Write a cover philosophy that describes what you want your cover to con-sistently say to readers, and develop plenty of examples to show how that philosophy will translate onto the page. Having the philosophy spelled out is of paramount im-portance in establishing a look—one that your readers identify as "uniquely you." In addition, it defines a common language for those involved in cover decisions and re-duces the "I like/I don't like" discussions that can take place.

Realtor® *Magazine's* cover philosophy calls for a strong, singular image that—combined with the primary cover line—can be "read" within a couple of seconds. We've opted primarily for full-bleed photography but agreed that type treatment cov-ers are acceptable for certain issues. We've specified a clear hierarchy (to differentiate primary and secondary cover lines) and a strict architecture, with secondary cover

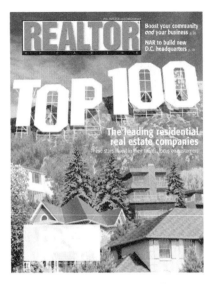

From National Association of Realtors®. Reprinted by permission of editor.

From National Association of Realtors®. Reprinted by permission of editor.

Toward a strong image. One way to grab readers' attention is to move away from busy images and use shorter, bolder cover lines.

lines and other text pushed toward the margins to create simple sight-lines and leave maximum space for the image.

Having a strong cover philosophy that all parties agree to will go a long way toward helping your magazine pass the gutter test.

Color Palette

There's a reason for the "golden" in "The Golden Arches." Color is one of the most effective ways to brand a product—including your magazine. In order to create a color identity, define a specific range of colors you want to use. Your palette doesn't have to be limiting. *Realtor® Magazine's* color palette includes 42 colors—seven shades each of neutral, red, orange, yellow, green, blue, and purple—but we use only a few of those shades most often. One of the reds we've labeled our "signature red." It's used on key elements throughout the magazine, including occasionally on our nameplate (the only alternative we allow to white) and on tabs that label every standard page.

Step 6: *Create page designs.* With the foundation of your book complete, you can begin designing pages. Create templates for key pages in the publication. Start with the folio lines. They should be on every page except the cover and full-page, full-bleed ads. Show cover, department, column, masthead, and table of contents treatments. Include repeating and "signature" elements such as page headers, tabs, "more information" boxes, pop-quotes, sidebars, end marks, and the like.

Designing Core Editorial Pages

Your magazine is a business tool—and your readers' professional reading time is probably short. Your readers may be paying a subscription price or receiving your magazine free as part of an industry-specific controlled circulation list or as a benefit of membership in a trade or professional organization. Either way, they won't give you their time if they don't quickly see a benefit. Therefore, it's imperative that your design make the editorial accessible by giving you multiple ways to telegraph its reader benefit.

Here's how we did that with *Realtor® Magazine*. The main signature element we incorporated onto our core pages was a tab, in our signature red, that appears in the top left corner of each page. It contains a label—Law, Selling, Buyer's Guide—followed by a kicker that sits above the headline and gives readers specific information about the story's subject. A department page might open like this:

Red Tab: Law
Kicker: LIABILITY INSURANCE
Headline: Proper coverage is critical

That combination makes it easy for readers to flip through or scan the book to find the sections and topics they're most interested in reading. When there's more information available to readers online, we hang an explanation off the red tab. That way,

From National Association of Realtors®. Reprinted by permission of editor.

From National Association of Realtors®. Reprinted by permission of editor.

Striving for impact. Images and headlines are made bolder to communicate core messages quickly.

readers become accustomed to looking to the tab for online resources. Like a strong cover philosophy, a good core editorial design is essential to passing the gutter test.

If there's one section where you'll want to break the rules of your core design, it's in your front-of-book department (alternatively known as the grab bag, potpourri, or news section). It generally consists of a different mix of elements than the rest of the publication, and the look should reflect that. For *Realtor*® *Magazine's* "Front Lines" section, we developed a distinctive nameplate to open the section, used a blue tab as a variation on the red tabs that appear throughout the book, and created a layout that allows for multiple elements on a page. Because Front Lines is focused on news and trends, a reminder of our online daily news updates hangs off the blue tabs on each page. In addition, we designed the entire Front Lines section as strong single pages to allow plenty of space for full-page, far-forward ads.

Designing Features

You'll want to create several samples of feature articles. Features should stand apart from your core pages. Typically, larger headlines, large opening art, and possibly large-type leads are employed. For business editors, executing the clean distinction can sometimes be easier said than done. Business publications are typically bound by strict ad-edit ratios, so it may feel extravagant to commit to features with 150-point headlines and full-page art treatments when you're barely squeezing editorial into the book. However, you need to ensure that readers see the clear visual shift. Including a discussion of art and layout in the planning stages of every feature will yield huge results.

Highlighting Value-Added Copy

One thing that has traditionally distinguished business books—but has been adopted by many consumer titles—is a focus on service journalism. We tell readers how to do their jobs better. And there are ways design can help us do that more effectively. Whether you're designing core pages or features, be sure to create attractive ways to break out value-added information—for example, five key points of the article, a step-by-step guide, quotes that sum up a person's business philosophy, or a paragraph on how a new law will impact your readers' business. Stock art is plentiful these days—and it's easily accessible via the Web and stock CDs. However, publication designers Ron Reason and Mario Garcia, who worked on the most recent redesign of *The Wall Street Journal,* say a good value-added breakout will ultimately serve your busy readers better than a piece of art with only a tangential connection to the subject.

Be prepared to explain how your design choices build on your foundation and follow from the brief you prepared in Step 3. Once your designs are complete, you can create standing templates that include the recurring elements.

Step 7: *Mock up an entire "dummy" issue of the publication.*   When you're presenting your design choices to your publisher, editorial director, and staff, it's a good idea to post a full dummy issue on a wall, in the order the pages will appear in the magazine, so your audience can get a sweeping view of the book. The pages should include:

- sample art, characteristic of art/photo choices you'd use
- real headlines to show that your headline design works with real editorial in your magazine
- real copy if you have the editorial resources to create samples of the new content

It's also a good idea to create a dummy issue, which can be accomplished economically by pasting a set of the mocks over the pages of an existing issue. This allows a "flip through" test to demonstrate how your pacing works and how your design holds up against the advertising.

Your dummy issue marks a good point to debut the new design to your staff and key advertisers. This first mock execution of the new design will undoubtedly raise issues you'll need to address. In our 2002 redesign, we caught some problems with proposed ad sizes and were able to make the necessary adjustments before production started on the first issue.

Step 8: *Put the first issue into production.*   Build extra time into your normal production schedule to allow for copy fitting issues and other first-time new-design challenges. For *Realtor® Magazine's* recent redesign, we added three weeks to our schedule. Also, as the new pages were produced, we posted color copies on a board so the whole staff could see the work in progress, and we could fix inconsistencies along the way.

Step 9: *Assess your work.*   Conduct monthly "post mortems" of each issue. This can be done between the editor, managing editor, art director, and graphic designer, or you can involve all the editorial and design staff. Do this religiously for the first six months, and then you can ease off to whatever frequency seems right to you. The point of these sessions is to make sure you're executing the redesign in a disciplined fashion and to make adjustments to design elements that aren't working out as you'd hoped. Resist the urge to tweak your new design too much. Live with it for a while and let the readers get used to it.

Reader feedback is important too. Don't count on readers writing in to tell you how great the new design is (though such letters are great!). Plan some formal way to solicit reader feedback within three-to-six months of your launch. We sought feedback through a reader survey that we published in the magazine and posted at our Web site.

Keeping Decision-Makers in the Loop

There are five critical points for bringing decision-makers into the process.

1. *Review of existing research, mission, and redesign brief.* **Goal:** Reach a consensus on who your readers are and how your redesign will serve them better than your current design.

What do you think? Ultimately, it's your readers who decide whether a publication redesign works. Give readers a few months to absorb a redesign and then ask them whether the new look is effective. To improve your chances of generating a broad response from your readers, offer a modest incentive. Here the incentive is a mug branded with the magazine logo. Use the feedback as a starting point for refining your redesign over the next several months.

From National Association of Realtors®. Reprinted by permission of editor.

2. *Review of your new core editorial.* **Goal:** Reach a consensus on the ideal editorial mix to achieve your mission.

Note: Steps 1 and 2 can be combined into a single meeting with decision makers.

3. *Review of design foundation.* **Goal:** Reach a consensus on the "architecture" for your design. If you do a good job of selling the foundation, reaching consensus on actual page templates should be a relative breeze.

4. *Review of page designs.* **Goal:** Reach a consensus on packaging and presentation. At this stage, applying the foundation you've created, you should be able to show decision makers mock layouts of every page—the cover, table of contents and masthead pages, every column and department, classified advertising pages, and several features.

5. *Tweaks.* Along the way, you, your editorial director, your publisher, and other editors will very likely suggest refinements to your page designs. Leave yourself a few weeks after your pages designs are finalized to make tweaks and have them reviewed and approved.

Concluding Information

Five Ways to Sell Your Ideas to Decision Makers

1. Schedule a formal meeting.   At each of the five approval stages, you should meet face-to-face with decision makers to pitch your recommendations and get feedback. Invite the right people: only decision makers, not your entire editorial staff.

2. Before the meeting, create a memo that outlines the main points you plan to make.   Writing the memo helps you make concrete exactly what you're recommending and why. If you're presenting your "picture" of the readers, include bullet points from recent research that support your picture. When you're proposing a new philosophy for your covers, spell out what the new philosophy will achieve. If you can send the memo to decision makers a day before your formal meeting, you'll signal that you've thought through your proposal and give them time to prepare questions.

3. Have visuals on hand to support your recommendations.   For example, if you currently have an illustrated cover but want to switch to photography, create examples of what your cover would look like with photography. If a change in body copy would make better use of your page, create a representation that shows a column of your current font against a column of your recommended font.

4. Set aside time, if necessary, to show your explorations.   Having the design options you've discarded at the ready can help you deflect decision maker objections. ("Yes, we looked at a larger type, but here's what we ran into." "We considered several serif faces for our logo but felt they weren't capturing the message we want to convey to our readers. Take a look.") This also demonstrates the level of energy and care you put into your final recommendations.

5. Be flexible.   It's one thing to deflect objections and its another to reject them. Listen to the feedback you're getting in meetings and don't be afraid to change course on a recommendation. Publishers and editorial directors typically have a keen understanding of reader and advertiser concerns and often have good ideas, too!

See chapter exercise at the back of this book.

Trade Show Coverage

4

It's Showtime, Folks

Robert Grace and Donald Loepp

Every industry has them. They're trade shows, and they're crucial to professionals. The events spotlight innovative products and services, and they serve as marketplaces for professionals to network, conduct business, and generate ideas.

To be a credible journalistic force in your industry, trade publication editors must cover such events thoroughly. The events are crucial for editors to stay on top of the industry they write about and to stock up on content ideas and sources.

The news generated at these events pose a terrific challenge for editors, certainly for those who are responsible for producing "a show daily," those special-purpose newspapers that share a parent publication's brand identity and deliver daily event coverage to attendees.

The value of a show daily to your readers and advertisers is directly proportional to the effort invested to produce it. If you approach the task casually, pre-writing much of the copy and plugging in only a few news stories and photos each day, readers may not put much stock into the publication's value.

But if you attack the project with gusto, organizing the project into a hard-hitting, vital news daily, you reinforce the value proposition of the parent publication and treat yourself to a challenging, but rewarding, opportunity.

How do you create a vital show daily? It's vital to be focused and proactive, especially when the trade show is large, involving thousands of square feet of exhibition space and hundreds of educational sessions.

Planning Your On-Site Coverage

For starters, show dailies require clear communication and finely honed coordination between all segments of your operation—advertising, marketing, editorial, production, and distribution—and allow little margin for error. After all, you can do a great job reporting and laying out pages on deadline and the publication can be expertly printed—and none of it matters if the issues don't make it into readers' hands the next morning. Logistics matter greatly, since an unforeseen event can render your

Robert Grace has been editor of Plastics News *since its launch in 1989, and assumed the additional titles of associate publisher in 1999 and conference director in 2000. Donald Loepp joined* Plastics News *in 1991 as a reporter and became managing editor in 1995.*

efforts moot. This possibility demands you approach your planning systematically. Get your plan in writing.

The Content Trap

It's tempting to sidestep risk when planning and executing a trade show daily newspaper by falling back on heavy use of pre-written filler copy. This editorial material—lengthy exhibitor lists and company-provided blurbs about what's on display at their booths—has its uses, and also provides the pages the publisher needs to attract advertisers. But the copy is unlikely to offer much value to readers, and it typically ends up as show-hall litter.

What makes show dailies compelling is the same thing that can make the parent publication compelling—well-executed, timely, and original content, punctuated by thoughtful reporting insights and analysis, and illustrated by quality photographs of people and events. But make no mistake, producing such content in hours, as opposed to the days or weeks you typically get on a regular publication, takes a well-thought-out strategy and a dedicated, enthusiastic staff.

If done properly, though, the payback is extensive: important information to your readers, value to your advertisers, profit to your publisher's bottom line, and a journalistic rush to your editorial staff—all while enhancing your publication's brand.

It certainly has meant all the above to *Plastics News,* a weekly publication covering the plastics industry, which exercises its show-daily muscles every three years at the huge, 90,000-attendee National Plastics Exposition. At NPE 2000, we delivered five issues (396 tabloid folio pages total) to attendees in five days—our regular Monday *Plastics News* issue with a special slot for show news, three midweek show dailies, plus early distribution on Friday at the show of our following Monday's weekly edition. The three dailies in 2000 each contained 22 tabloid pages of editorial content and 50 pages of advertising, and the three dailies in 2003 were of a similar size.

Plastics News has 60,000 weekly subscribers. For an event the size of NPE, we typically print an extra 20,000 copies of our full-run Monday issue for distribution at the expo. The print runs for our dailies taper off slightly as the week progresses, from 20,000 copies on Tuesday to about 12,000 on Thursday. We then distribute an extra 12,000 copies on Friday of the following week's regular issue. We employ a team of locally hired temporary helpers, dressed in *PN*-provided uniforms and trained by our marketing director just prior to the show, to hand out issues to attendees at various strategic entrances throughout the complex. We also arrange with the show organizers and local unions to distribute issues each morning on the shuttle buses bringing attendees to the conference from their hotels.

While on site in 2000, our 11 reporters and correspondents filed 113 stories, accounting for more than half of the 2,600-plus editorial column inches that we published in the three midweek show dailies. The American Society of Business Publication Editors recognized the effort by presenting *Plastics News* with its 2000 national gold award for best on-site trade show coverage in the country that year.

Live, from the newsroom. Timely and broad coverage separates news-oriented show dailies from pre-packaged marketing publications. To work effectively with the highly compressed editorial turnaround times of a show daily, editors must assemble a news-gathering team and devise an editing and production process well in advance of the industry show. During showtime, flexibility is key. Establish an environment in which reporters can identify and report on news effectively while also capturing must-cover events.

Plastics News/Crain Communications Inc. with permission.

Not all our daily efforts have been on such a grand scale. We also, for example, have produced 16-page dailies at smaller events. But the tactics and skills needed to deliver strong show coverage are very similar, regardless of folio size.

What Content to Include

One of the first and most obvious questions an editor faces when mapping out a show daily project is each issue's content. Certainly, circumstances vary from expo to expo, and these differences must be taken into account when mulling the options. For instance, most trade shows offer every attendee a directory that includes full exhibitor listings and booth numbers, and schedules of any accompanying conferences. If that's the case, then what's the point of reprinting such information in each issue of your daily?

Strive to deliver real news and solid, entertaining features. Providing daily attendance numbers, for example, especially when you compare them with same-day or show-to-date numbers from the same event the last time it was held, offers an independent, statistical yardstick by which to measure activity. Exhibitors are always interested in attendance figures.

At the same time, don't ignore the allure of people pictures and so-called wild art (unposed photographs) that help capture readers' attention, brighten a gray page, and consume some of the editorial real estate you're charged with filling. Such art can be effective when it captures an exhibit or event from the show floor that many of your show-going readers may have witnessed in person the previous day.

All *Plastics News* reporters carry cameras and take their own photographs, yet we struggle to take enough photographs to fill the pages of our show dailies. To help us fill the hole, for each NPE show we bring in a professional news photographer. It's important to find a photographer who knows how to stage-manage executives into visually interesting positions and is careful at recording names and caption information, while still delivering quality images on excruciatingly tight deadlines. Strong photos can visually transform your daily issues, and improvements in digital technology are making it easier to incorporate photos in your publications.

Plotting Your Game Plan

Of course, nobody can reasonably produce a large-folio show daily each day, on-site, from scratch. You need prewritten copy, ready artwork, partially completed early forms, a reasonably sized news hole, and a sensible game plan. The key is to try to keep even that prewritten copy as fresh and useful as possible.

There are some simple tactics you can use to help achieve that, and this is where advance planning becomes crucial.

For starters, you need to stockpile stories and art well in advance of the show. These can be news features, market trend stories, product news, Q&A interviews, profiles of executives or companies—whatever has value and some shelf life. As a safeguard, we also prepare some filler copy (such as a spotlight on industry events) that can go on a daily page if absolutely necessary to meet a deadline, but we hope to never have to use it.

We include our usual editorial page in our show dailies, and weeks in advance solicit guest-written opinion columns on broad industry issues to help fill out that space. We strive to focus on topics that will draw on hot-button themes or talking points during the exhibition.

Many trade shows feature a conference program or show guide. These sometimes can provide good news fodder, but again you'll do better to do advance legwork. Scout out the program, contact those speakers who look like they might be addressing newsworthy topics and solicit their photos plus advance copies of their presentations, or perhaps interview them before the event. But, of course, don't write up advance stories based on provided speeches without attending the talk to make sure the presenter both shows up and sticks to the script. Additionally, the question-and-answer session afterwards typically yields the most interesting news nuggets.

Making the Most of Your Time

For an event the size of an NPE, which in 2000 had more than 2,000 exhibitors and covered in excess of 1 million square feet of exhibit space, editors get inundated with invitations to press conferences, receptions, and personal appointments on booths, dinners, etc. Some such events have editorial value, while others can be a waste of time—and your reporters simply can't afford to waste time when they're knee-deep in a daily.

For starters, appoint one person well before the event to coordinate and prioritize all incoming invitations and reporter assignments. Be sure to ask questions before accepting invitations to press conferences and events during the show, to try to determine their true newsworthiness. Assess with caution those who promise "big news" at a press event, but won't tip their hand—even on an embargoed basis—about what it is. We generally insist on some prior indication of the news to be announced, or we won't guarantee we will cover it. You've got leverage. Use it.

When it comes to managing your time at the show, prearrange and reconfirm on-site interviews (and, if appropriate, photo shoots) with those executives you definitely wish to see, and tell others that you'll do your best to get there, without necessarily committing to a specific time. The aim is to get the best news bang for your time investment.

Don't limit your potential pool of interview targets to executives at exhibiting companies. Contact key sources or companies of interest well in advance, to determine if and when they may be at the event, and then try to nail down appointments. This can be particularly useful when trying to connect with foreign visitors or delegations, which your reporters might normally not have easy access to.

Also, be aware that sometimes the best news leads reside with officials who are wandering the aisles at a show. Make sure your reporters make an effort to read visitors' name badges, and introduce themselves to worthy news targets, regardless of whether those individuals are exhibiting or not. Such extra efforts increase the likelihood that reporters will find and generate solid copy for the next day's issue.

Other News-Gathering Tips

Months prior to a large show, we obtain from the show organizers a copy of the exhibitor database, including contact information. We send an e-mail or fax blast to each exhibitor with a single-page survey form, asking each of them to tell us what they plan to introduce or announce that is truly new at the show. We request photos and ask for details about any press conferences or special events that their firm is planning during show week. This information helps us to fill the three show-preview issues that we publish before each NPE, while also providing useful planning intelligence.

Our editorial troops are so strapped for time during show week that we do whatever we can to streamline the process for receiving news tips, while also attempting to minimize time-wasting activities. At each NPE, and we set up a temporary newsroom in the lower level of the exhibition complex and we don't publicize its whereabouts. We don't want to deal with sources that wander in to chat, complain, or pitch a story.

Planning and Preparing

One of the first decisions you need to make when you decide to produce a show daily is whom you will bring to cover the show, and what they will do. For *Plastics News,* it's almost a matter of bringing every available body. The fact that most of our reporters and correspondents have experience at daily newspapers or newswires is a tremendous advantage. They're used to reporting and delivering breaking news. They quickly shift back into daily mode, and get energized by the challenge. Another major advantage: daily newspaper reporters tend to be quick learners, able to make sense of complicated topics and put them in language that anyone can understand, and they have a great instinct for recognizing real news.

Magazine staffs without such experience also can make the transition successfully, but it may be more intimidating, at least the first time around. That makes planning all the more important.

The *Plastics News* managing editor plays the key logistical role in the run-up to and execution of our big daily projects. Come show time, the managing editor is the first editorial staffer to head to the exhibition center, usually arriving on the Thursday before NPE starts the following Monday. He works with technical staff to ensure the on-site newsroom gets set up as we want it.

Who Belongs on the Travel Team?

1. The people who will report the news and take the pictures.
2. The people who will give the stories a first edit, ask key questions, and then get the copy into production.

Why do you need to decide the travel team first? Because that gives the reporters plenty of time to get up to speed on what they'll be covering at the show. Good reporting takes preparation. Reporters need time to identify the major players on their beats, and to understand the important trends and issues.

Tips for Reporters to Prepare for the Big Show

1. Assign them responsibility to cover their show daily beat in pre-show issues.
2. Give them time to learn about the companies.
3. Ask them for trend stories they plan to tackle.
4. Get them involved in planning visits and interviews before and during the show.

This won't apply to every publication, but in our case the reporters who cover our show daily often must handle beats that they don't track on a regular basis. Most of our reporters devote the majority of their time covering our primary readers—plastics processing companies. So we traditionally have structured our beats according to end markets, such as packaging, medical, construction, and automotive.

But at the show, most of the coverage revolves around suppliers to our readers. In our case, that's primarily from machinery and materials suppliers. It's far too much for our regular machinery and resin reporters to handle, so we ask all of our reporters to become experts on a particular segment of the supply sector.

Here's a mistake that we made early in our show daily experience that you can learn from: In some of our first efforts we gave most of the responsibility for handling pre-show coverage to a handful of correspondents who were happy to do as much of it as they could because they were paid by the column inch. That generated plenty of material for our pre-show issues, with most of the copy consisting of new-product briefs. But the problem came later, when the other reporters didn't have a well-defined beat where they had built up a level of expertise.

If you have everyone running and covering beats, you may have a problem. People expect to go to your booth and find someone interested in their news. But if all of your reporters are busy visiting exhibitors and attending news conferences, you'll have no one at the booth to take their stories. You can get great stories from these booth visitors. Our editor is well known in the industry and perfect in this role. He can spot VIP booth visitors likely to have news to share, and he's prepared to handle most any kind of on-the-spot interview. Maybe your publication has a senior editor or columnist who can fill the same role.

In addition, we keep distinctively colored forms, or "tip sheets," at our booth that anyone who is seeking coverage can fill out. The form asks key questions: what sort of news they have, how and when to reach them at the show, including booth numbers, cell phone number, etc. A *PN* representative on our booth shuttles those completed forms down to our McCormick newsroom about once an hour, where we quickly scan and prioritize them and, if desired, assign a reporter or photographer to act on them. It's a good idea to stress on the tip sheet that completing such a form does not ensure a reporter will call on the company, or that a story will be generated from the lead—it's always wise to damp down expectations.

Who on Your Staff Doesn't Come to the Show?

1. The editors who will do the final edits and lay out pages.
2. At least one reporter to handle all the industry news not happening at the show.

Reporters don't have time to turn in a story and then sit around waiting for questions when you're producing a show daily. So your editors need to move quickly, at least on the high-priority stories. You'll still need to contact reporters on the fly with urgent, deadline questions. Pagers help, and cell phones are even better. They're also invaluable for reaching reporters to give them breaking news assignments.

When we first did NPE dailies, we packed up all of our copy editors and brought them to Chicago. Basically we had to. But that's no longer necessary. Now we have our reporters working in a temporary newsroom in the basement of the exhibition center, and we send our stories and photos to our "home" newsroom via e-mail. The copy desk handles the layout and sends the pages electronically to our printer. We're able to send our last stories to our home office by early evening, and the finished newspapers arrive at the show well before the show opens the next day.

One important aside: If you split your editorial team between cities, as we do, don't forget to overnight (or ask your printer to overnight) a few completed daily issues back to the copy desk at your home office each day when you receive them at the show. Those members of your team sweated hard to produce those issues and are as eager to see them as you are—and it's easy due to fatigue and deadline pressures to forget this detail.

There's always news that breaks away from the show floor during NPE. And just because it doesn't happen on-site doesn't mean our show daily readers don't care. But

This just in. Create a place for late-breaking news, including news generated outside the show. Maintain a staff person at the home office to keep watch on news generated outside the show and to research news tips that on-site reporters can't accommodate. The off-site reporter can also answer queries from the on-site copy desk.

Plastics News/Crain Communications Inc. with permission.

how do you report this kind of news when all of your reporters are up to their eyeballs covering the show? Here's how: We have an experienced former staffer come into the home office to check the incoming mail and faxes for important breaking stories. This person is also available to make calls on non-show-related news tips we might feed to her from Chicago and to research questions for our copy desk on show news.

In addition, we depend on our network of international correspondents to cover news in their regions. We let them know in advance when and where we'll be producing dailies, and make sure they're aware of the special deadline considerations involved with handling breaking news that week. Our phone, fax, and e-mail links keep us in communication all the time.

The Rest of Your Team

When you depend on technology as much as we do, that puts a lot of pressure on your production team. Their cooperation is essential. We make sure our production department has a lot of advance notice so they can schedule their people to handle our workload, and be on call to handle emergencies around the clock during show week.

The same applies to our computer gurus. Make sure you're covered with someone who can reset your modems and fix your systems if anything goes wrong—especially if you're renting or borrowing equipment you're not used to using. If you're anything like us, you'll be asking your hardware to hold a lot more photos and other large files than it typically handles. Make sure you, and it, are prepared to deal with whatever might arise.

Planning Keys

1. Stay flexible.
2. Plan to cover what you need to cover.
3. Have trends and questions in mind.

Companies come to the show with big announcements: mergers, joint ventures, significant new products and the like. With proper preparation, that should be the easy stuff to cover. The main players are there for in-person interviews and photos, and their competitors and customers, plus expert consultants, are just a few steps away.

It's the stories from companies that don't plan big news events or don't put together splashy press kits that require legwork.

Hardest of all are the stories that exhibitors and attendees would prefer to keep quiet. Trade shows are great places to hear rumors, so keep your ears peeled and be prepared to check out a dozen news tips—including a few that will turn out to be true! Once, one of our better show stories was one that quashed an untrue rumor about a major supplier declaring bankruptcy.

Pre-Written Coverage

Although our show dailies are known for their on-site content, certain kinds of news should be covered in advance of the show. When companies contact us in advance with big news that they want to get into our daily, we usually try to get the scoop right away. That gives the exhibitor a chance to talk away from deadline pressure. It also gives your reporter time to cover the story thoroughly, and it gives the editor a chance to plan art and to give the story proper play.

Sometimes, though, you need to press companies to provide you with their news in advance. Many firms (or their public relations agents) resist this, thinking they'll make a bigger splash by being secretive until their on-site press conference at the show. In such cases, for the above-noted reasons, some re-education is needed.

As a rule, we avoid agreeing to embargoed release dates on stories for *Plastics News,* but we are willing to play that game for show dailies. It also sometimes is the only way to get a company to agree to release timely news details in advance. Occasionally, a PR person cautions that they don't want to be seen to be playing favorites by releasing information early to one publication, but not to others. Our typical response to that is: "If our competitors cared about your news as much as we do, they'd be asking you for your information, too." Exclusives come to those who pursue them.

Leading Up to Coverage

Don't neglect trend stories. They serve many purposes, including providing:

1. your reporters good icebreaker questions with which to open their interviews;
2. guaranteed interesting content for your daily should you hit a slow patch in breaking news;

3. great content for post-show issues if breaking news crowds the trend stories out of the dailies.

Look beyond typical trends: legislative issues, trade and currency changes, environmental impacts, training and worker availability, the economy, financial condition of trade groups, worker health and safety, women- and minority-owned companies, research and development spending, materials prices, and productivity issues.

Have your reporters pick a topic relative to their beat and interests, do their homework in advance (including tracking down relevant data and experts), and then finish their work at the show. The story can be topped up with fresh quotes gathered there, and illustrated with original art taken on-site.

For a complicated subject, it may make sense to do the meat of the reporting and writing in advance, then wrap up the reporting with a show-produced sidebar. Writing on deadline for the show daily, you're better off having reporters trying to write shorter, breaking news-type stories rather than long features.

Interviews

With that in mind, here's a word about the handling of interviews in the question-and-answer format. They certainly can have a place in your show daily, but we recommend keeping them short—or doing them in advance. Trade shows are fantastic places to track down and interview top executives—the kind of people who, if you ask the right questions, just about anything they say will be of interest to your readers. Long Q&As are very time consuming to transcribe (most of our reporters tape-record interviews only for Q&A features or to cover major speeches). Also, keep your reader in mind! They're more likely to tackle a shorter story in a show daily than a long feature. It's a challenge to your reporters to write a lot of short, interesting stories, but we guarantee that those are the ones that will be read.

Keeping Your Cool

The first time we did show dailies, we panicked a little. We filled some pages with pre-written copy because the copy desk had some free time and was itching to fill pages, and our reporters were a little slow in filing show news. Preventing that is a big part of your job. You need to know what stories are coming, where they should go, how long they'll be, and you have to be prepared to handle them quickly. You're the traffic cop that needs to keep everything running smoothly, to prevent jams, and to make sure you save space for the important news. Quick decision-making and flexibility is essential.

After the Show

A brief word about our post-show coverage. It's important to remember that, no matter how large an event, many readers will not attend the exhibition. Therefore, important stories that appear first in your show daily must be republished in one of your later, full-run editions. Though it means some duplication with previous daily coverage, we repackage in the issue that we distribute at the show on Friday those hottest stories from the week's dailies.

We also schedule thematic, post-show coverage for the four to six weeks following the event. We challenge our reporters to reassess the various breaking news they covered on their beats, and to develop market-trend stories that add context and analysis to their initial short, sharp stories. You might also be able to use new or different photos or graphics to illustrate the same story the second time around.

Reader Feedback

Once, a reader told one of our editors, "I love *Plastics News*. It's the *People* magazine of the plastics industry." We were a little crestfallen. We think of ourselves as the *Wall Street Journal* of plastics. Why *People?* He explained that he meant it as a compliment. He reads both *Plastics News* and *People* for pleasure. Those are the magazines he took along to read on airplanes, and this person did a lot of traveling. Most of our stories are short, well-written, and packed with information, he said, and he knew right away whether it was a topic he was interested in reading.

We like to produce show dailies that people will talk about, take with them back to the hotel or office at the end of the day, and look forward to reading. Every time we do a daily we find things we're proud of, as well as things we'd like to do better next time—which brings us to another key component: continuous improvement.

Shortly after completing your show-daily project, but after you've rested, convene a meeting of your editorial staff and review the experience. Discuss what procedures worked well, what didn't, and why. Suggest ways to do things better. Take copious notes, then type them up and file them where you can find them when you get ready to start planning your next project. This allows you not only to capture important impressions while they are still fresh, but helps to institutionalize some of that vital knowledge in case any key members of your staff leave before the next big show.

And, last but not least, be sure to acknowledge and reward your staff for the extra effort they made before and during the event. Throw a post-show party, reward all involved, then get back to your desks and start planning the next big project!

Concluding Information

Daily Production Schedule

The following provides a sense of our show-daily production schedule. Though the 72-page dailies carried the equivalent of 50 tabloid-size pages of advertising, its 22 tabloid pages of editorial content stretched over a total of 36 folio pages. In other words, any page that was not 100 percent display or classified advertising required editorial staff involvement to complete.

For the NPE 2000 show, this was our Monday schedule for shipping pages to the printer for our Tuesday show daily (all times were Eastern Standard Time, where our Akron copy desk was located, which was one hour later than the time in our Chicago show-daily newsroom):

Monday show-daily production schedule:

9:30 a.m. – 7 pages
10:30 a.m. – 8 pages
11:30 a.m. – 3 pages
12:30 p.m. – 3 pages
1:30 p.m. – 3 pages
2:30 p.m. – 1 page
3:30 p.m. – 2 pages
4:30 p.m. – 2 pages
5:30 p.m. – 2 pages
6:30 p.m. – 2 pages
7:30 p.m. – Final 3 pages

Given that the show started at 9 a.m. on Monday, we obviously had to fill some of that day's early-form pages with prewritten copy. But even with these tight deadlines, we maximized the content from the show. Our Tuesday daily included 22 stories and three photos that we generated on-site in Chicago.

The deadlines for our Wednesday daily were similar, but since we had more show hours to report on, our on-site content expanded. The Wednesday daily contained 32 on-site-generated stories, plus 13 show-floor photos.

The numbers for Thursday speak for themselves: The daily included 59 Chicago-generated stories, plus 11 show-floor photos. Translation: a full three-quarters of that day's issue was reported and written on-site. Incidentally, we simultaneously completed production that Thursday on the final forms for the following Monday's normal, 56-page, full-run issue, which we distributed to show-goers on Friday morning. We gave the entire copy desk the day off on Friday.

The On-Site Attendee Survey

Consider working with a partner to survey attendees each day at the show about crucial industry issues, and then turning the results into stories or infographics for your dailies. Such a project can range from the simple to the ambitious. If anything, we have been too ambitious with this in the past, and devoted too much of our reporters' time to gathering comments to weave into a major trend story supported by the daily survey's results. So now we're scaling back. But there still can be value even in simple surveys, if done properly.

Craft a series of topical, newsworthy questions. Contract with another party—possibly an industry company or association looking to benefit from some editorial daily exposure—to manage the logistics of intercepting attendees, asking them a brief set of questions, collating the responses and delivering them to you in a timely manner each afternoon of the show. Some firms may be willing to pay professional survey-takers to handle that task; others may choose to handle it themselves.

Since you already know the questions and possible responses, you can create a template for infographics in advance, and simply plug in the numbers when you get them. That gives you an instant color graphic drawn from show-floor responses to timely questions. The results may be unscientific, but they can be interesting, nonetheless.

Factoring in the Internet

As with most news organizations today, the Internet is a vital delivery channel for *Plastics News,* and it can play a key role in your trade-show coverage. We already update our *Plastics News* Web site several times daily with breaking news.

During show week, with every member of our staff fully committed to show-daily production, it can be challenging to give the site attention. But we make time to do so since many in the industry will look to our Web site that week for breaking news from the trade show. We also display the site at our own trade-show booth, and nothing is a better indicator of our news-gathering operation than to have a story online about an event we covered earlier that same day.

Some six to eight weeks before the show, we launch a special, advertiser-sponsored NPE section on our Web site that includes preview stories, features, conference programs, hotel and logistical information, and links to organizer-provided exhibitor lists and registration forms. We then post all NPE-related stories in that section before, during, and after the event, and leave the section online well after the show ends. In 2000, our online NPE section was both profitable for us and valuable for our readers and sponsors, as it featured more than 260 original business-news and product stories, relevant editorials, columns, cartoons and the like. Also, given the global nature of the Internet, this effort provides us with a means of delivering the fruits of our labors to a larger audience.

E-Delivery of News to the Show Floor

Our daily news coverage at the NPE show in June 2003 took a new twist, when for the first time we delivered scrolling news headlines and one-line story summaries to show-goers via electronic display screens mounted above the show floor.

This developed from a project whereby we agreed to organize two dozen product-locator computer terminals clustered at strategic points throughout the exhibition center on which attendees could search for exhibitors and types of products and services, and print out the results on the spot. We mounted large, flat-screen displays a few feet above these computer clusters and used them to display headlines and daily conference and event schedule information that would be of value to attendees.

The plan called for using existing networking systems at the exhibition center to link these screens via a local mini-network throughout the complex, to enable us to easily post periodic updates.

The electronic display is another medium by which we can deliver timely news to the industry, reinforcing our effort to be our industry's key news source.

Special Supplements

5

Making a Parent Publication Proud

Regina McGee

Special supplements are stand-alone, single-topic publications that build off the brand identity of a parent publication. And they constitute a major part of trade journalism.

For publishers, they're an opportunity to deliver specialized editorial content for readers, while extending an existing publication's brand and advertising possibilities. For editors, they're an opportunity to dig deep into a topic and explore creative editorial and design ideas that are rarely possible on their regular publication.

Supplements differ widely, from state-of-the industry reports to analyses of the top issues or top companies in an industry. But they all aim to capitalize on an existing publication brand with content that is more focused than can typically be accommodated in a regular publication.

That said, there are a few things special supplements aren't:

Advertorials. Supplements must be editorially independent, and they must contain objective content. That's not to say advertorials can't be helpful to their readers. But because they lack an objective viewpoint, an advertorial can't be an editorial product.

Special sections. These are "editorially controlled special reports appearing within a calendar issue, and easily distinguished from regular features." The definition is from the American Society of Business Publication Editors. You can't tear out a special section and call it a supplement.

Special Issues. These are typically regular calendar issues with a focus on a single topic. By this measure, they're not a special supplement.

Best Practices

What distinguishes an effective from a less-than effective supplement are the same elements that distinguish a good trade publication. Tops on the list would be *value to readers*. No matter what the subject matter—diesel engines or surgical techniques—a really good supplement will be conceived and executed with reader take-away upper

---

Regina McGee, editor of Association Meetings, *a Primedia publication, has been a journalist and editor for 20 years.*

most in mind. It will help readers do their job better, save them money or time, or possibly all three. It will be timely and useful.

A good example: *CIO Insight,* a magazine for business information technology executives, produced "The Alignment Gap" in 2002 to help executives align their IT and business strategy. By including columns, features, case studies, and research statistics, the supplement gave readers a rich knowledge base to tap on a topic that is of critical importance to them. Despite the technical nature of the topic, the copy was readable and the design crisp and clean. Practically each one of its 100 pages had an interesting pull-quote or other graphic that helped engage the reader.

Moreover, an eight-page advertising insert that could very easily have been taken as editorial copy was labeled throughout as "Special Advertising Section." Not labeling this section would have diminished a great editorial product.

Hand-and-hand with reader value is *dimensionality of reporting.* An anniversary supplement that contains nothing but pictures and fascinating details of luminaries in an industry will not be as successful as one that adds other ingredients to the text, perhaps an analysis by one or more independent experts, or charts illustrating different trends, or a list of reference materials for readers.

Although it is not always possible, a supplement that has editorial *depth as well as breadth* has a greater impact with readers. Upshot: Your four- or eight- or ten-page supplement is likely not to offer as much heft as those that have larger folios with which to develop and explore a topic fully.

One would think it would go without saying that a good supplement is *carefully edited* and written in easy-to-understand language.

And finally, the supplement should have a *variety of sources,* and the sources should be credible. If you are just quoting your advertisers, you're not going to make the grade with readers.

Packaging Tips

Even more than with a regular publication, which readers approach with some familiarity, special supplements must be presented in a way that makes it clear what its content is all about. In this regard, nothing is more vital than how you approach your packaging. The cover must be compelling and informative and the heads descriptive.

Here's the cover head and deck of a supplement produced by the editors of *Construction Equipment:*

"Diesels in the crosshairs: how will new engines affect on- and off-road equipment and trucks?"

Okay, not the sexiest head and deck you're likely to see, but it gives the reader exactly what the supplement is about without wasting anyone's time—and that's better than being so clever with cover copy that the reader hasn't a clue what's inside.

It also helps to create a tagline under the logo on the cover summing up the aim of the content.

Here's the tagline for *Beyond Borders,* a supplement I edited on hosting association meetings abroad:

"Taking your meeting outside the United States."

That says it in a nutshell. And don't lose a great branding opportunity by failing to have the parent magazine's name or logo on the cover.

After the cover the table of contents is the most important page. Here's where the reader will turn to glean a quick understanding of what the supplement is about and whether it's worth one's scrutiny. The TOC should be designed for easy scanning, with the most important content elements getting the weightiest visual treatment.

The editors of *Convenience Store/Petroleum* do a nice job with the TOC page in a *2002 State of the Industry* report. Again, fancy graphics aren't necessary, just excellent readability.

Good heads, decks, and pull-quotes are critical throughout the issue, just as they are in a regular publication. Long blocks of uninterrupted type are never a good idea, since you want points of entry for readers with little inclination to read a full text. Sidebars and infographics keep readers' interest and help them digest the information in bits and pieces.

Ideas for Editorial Supplements

When planning supplements for your industry, start with what's already out there. If you can come up with an editorial product that readers need but can't find anywhere else, you've got the seeds for a winner. Here are some popular formats:

- State-of-the-industry reports: *Meetings & Conventions* produced an award-winning state of the industry supplement in 2002. The 56-page book made a high volume of data less daunting with easy-to-read charts, and used the text, for the most part, to analyze the data. This is critical. Giving the reader just the raw data without helping them make sense of it is to lose an opportunity to serve the reader. It is also tremendously helpful to start out by giving the reader an overview analysis.
- Anniversary supplements: What makes a good one? If they contain nothing but profiles of luminaries, they can get tiresome to read. Pictures contrasting past and present add a twist. Sidebars or infographics showing trends keep the reader moving along.
- Top 25 professionals or businesses: These have built-in appeal for readers. Each industry has its key and colorful personalities, and readers in that industry like to read about them. And everybody wants to know the inside scoop on success stories. *Federal Computer Week* did a nice job with its 2002 supplement *How They Stack Up.* It combined personality profiles, data tables, analyses, and very simple but effective typography.

- Niche markets: Focusing on the information needs of a segment of readership can be effective. *Beyond Borders* is an example. It focuses on the nuts-and-bolts of planning overseas events, a very different task from planning domestic events. Thus, it is distributed *only* to readers who plan events outside of the United States. What's more, advertisers love these targeted publications. It gives them a chance to reach a niche audience.

- Handbooks/how-to compendiums: Some tips for these types of supplements, which can easily get a bit dry: keep copy highly readable by using bullets, sidebars, and good infographics and captions; and above all, make sure it's information your audience really needs.

- Topical issues/special reports: This is an interesting supplement format. A good example is *Homeland Security,* published in 2002 by *Government Executive.* Obviously, the topic was of keen and timely interest to the parent magazine's readers.

- Career guides: Everybody wants to know how to get ahead in their careers. These supplements have to get beyond the obvious content, quote excellent sources, and be up-to-date. Having personal profiles of success stories is a nice human-interest touch. *Game Career Guide,* a 2002 supplement published by *Game Developer,* offered features on creating your own resume and demo reel, how to win the interview game, and how to choose the right education path. The 56-page supplement had a directory of schools, solid information on salaries, and a profile of a successful game developer.

- Salary studies: Up-to-date information and credible survey methodology are critical. Break up the data with personality profiles, trend analysis, and reference lists.

Concluding Information

The Online Supplement: An Idea Whose Time Has Come?

The Web creates expanded possibilities for supplements. *Purchasing Magazine* in 2002 produced *E-Auction Playbook II* as a 26-page supplement available only online in a PDF document. The supplement provided best practices and advice on central online auction matters, plus tips on hosting reverse auctions.

The fact that the playbook exits only online is an appropriate touch given the subject matter—e-auctions. But online supplements have untapped potential for other kinds of trade publications. The format provides a way to offer highly technical supplements, because of the amount of depth you can go into. The format is also attractive for supplements that might not have a large enough potential readership or advertising support to justify the production costs of a print product.

At the same time, online supplements that compile existing articles organized around a theme is a cost-effective way to populate your Web site and make a one-stop shopping experience for readers who have themed information needs.

Dos and Don'ts of Special Supplements

1. Don't call it a special supplement unless it is editorially independent and objective, and unless it is produced as a separate publication to a parent magazine. Ideally it should be mailed with regular issue.

2. Don't forget to add dimension and depth to your coverage by including reference material, infographics, and sidebars.

3. Don't neglect presentation. You don't have to spend a lot of money on graphics and art but you do have to create a product that invites the reader to jump into the issue.

4. Do pay close attention to heads, decks, and pull quotes. Try to give the reader more than one entry point on a page with, for example, a sidebar, graph, or pull quote.

5. Don't create a product that is so different in appearance from the parent publication that readers don't easily grasp the connection. You lose a branding opportunity by creating a product that is not easily linked with your magazine.

6. Hone the editorial mission. Create a tagline under the logo on the cover that gives readers an immediate idea of what the supplement is about.

7. Do produce a supplement that appears every year. This builds reader and advertiser loyalty. But make sure your content is fresh.

8. Don't use sources that aren't credible. Be careful about quoting too many sources from advertisers. Your goal should be to tap a variety of sources to prevent your supplement from singing a one-note song.

9. Do try to create a one-of-a-kind supplement that will not only enhance the parent magazine's branding, but also draw new advertising dollars.

Technical Editing I   6

Turning Experts into Writers

Paul Heney

The career path of engineers or other technical professionals doesn't typically wind its way through writing school, and yet these are the writers that trade editors rely on for much of the technical content in their publications. For that reason, how well editors translate technical submissions into engaging and useful articles for readers is a key test of a trade publication's strengths.

What are the factors that go into a successful collaboration between editors and expert contributors? There are more than you might think.

It's not enough for an editor to bring a skillful hand at rewriting to a contribution; given the resource constraints that trade publications characteristically face, few editors have the luxury to spend as much time as they'd like rewriting the work of technical experts. What's more, applying too heavy of a hand in editing can alienate contributors if the expectations of the contribution aren't carefully outlined upfront.

For these reasons and more, editors' successful collaboration with expert contributors begins and ends with relationship building. Put another way, the editing process begins long before editors have the submission in their hands; it begins in the article planning stage, with editors finding the right contributor for a piece, making the assignment clearly, identifying expectations, and then rewriting the piece as necessary to create an article that engages and enlightens readers.

But the relationship doesn't stop there. Given the nature of technical articles, presentation is a key editorial issue. Editors work with the technical expert to determine and then to execute the best way to convey information graphically.

Identifying and Compensating Expert Contributors

Finding the right expert is of particular concern when you're looking for someone to write a feature-length article, because these articles require considerable time commitment and sufficient writing and organizational skills to attack a subject fully. In addition to finding a person with knowledge of the technology, a passion for the subject is crucial. Without passion, a contributor can little hope to carry a subject through to its conclusion in a way that engages readers.

Trained as an engineer, Paul Heney, senior editor of Hydraulics & Pneumatics, *published by Penton Media in Cleveland, Ohio, is immediate past president of the American Society of Business Publication Editors.*

With this in mind, how do editors match the right person to the task? Each one approaches the task differently, but trade publication editors rely heavily on their contacts in the industry to identify experts to work with.

Trade Shows

"Our access to industry experts derives mainly from a large network we've developed through trade shows, conference and forum attendance, and through membership in the industry's professional trade organizations," says Dr. William J. Pike, editorial director of Houston-based *Hart's E&P*, an oil and gas exploration magazine.

Matt Halverson, managing editor of Kansas City-based *EC&M,* which covers the electrical construction and maintenance industries, looks for contributors even at trade shows he can't attend by pulling information on speakers from the press kits. "If the organizers of a trade show feel someone is well versed enough in a topic to present it in a technical session, chances are that he or she will be a good resource for us," says Halverson.

Existing Contributors

A publication's existing pool of contributing editors is another source, says Kathy Blomstrom, editor of *SQL Server* in Loveland, Colo., which covers the Microsoft SQL Server product line. These contributors are on top of industry trends and can help you get in touch with emerging industry leaders.

Web Forums

Blomstrom also monitors Web forums and newsgroups for participants who consistently give accurate and well-formed explanations, keep track of authors who have books out on the topics they're covering, and keep in contact with top consultants who are implementing leading-edge solutions.

Compensation

Finding experts is only half the battle, of course. The other half is converting them into contributors. Sometimes that means offering compensation, even if it's a modest stipend. But most of the time getting space in your magazine is all the inducement they need.

The reason for this is supply and demand. In most industries, having a technical feature byline is a coup for a company, which may buy reprints of the article or use it for marketing purposes. Additionally, having the byline suggests that XYZ Chemical Co. employs technical experts who are at the cutting edge of what's happening in the industry. To many companies, that is worth more than whatever stipend a publication can pay.

As it is, some companies provide a bonus or other incentive to induce employees to write for a trade magazine, and a few require high-ranking experts to do so once or twice per year.

The few publications that do compensate their expert contributors don't pay very much, typically $50 or $100.

SQL Server is one of these. It pays its contributors 40 cents to $1 per word, depending on several factors, including the writer's experience, technical reputation, and relationship with the magazine. Looking ahead, for some articles, the compensation may be a flat fee. "We're considering changing our pay scale for unsolicited articles to $200, a tee-shirt, a copy of our CD archive of back issues, and a subscription to the magazine," says Blomstrom.

Follow-Through

In spite of the pressure from the industry side for experts to get their work in a trade publication, the business publication editor will quickly find that as many as half of the articles promised fail to pan out. The most common reason is lack of time. Experts typically maintain a busy schedule and simply don't have the time they thought they would. Given this reality, editors must be prepared with other articles to draw on, requiring them to keep multiple irons in the fire at all times.

Getting an Expert Started on the Piece

Once you've matched a contributor to a topic, the next step is to get that expert thinking like a writer. Do that by asking them to think about the organizational pattern of what they are writing about. If they are writing about a piece of machinery, common enough in technical trade publications, a rough outline might look something like this.

- What does the machine do?
- Who uses it?
- How does it operate?
- What are its advantages and disadvantages over competitive machines?

Many technical magazines use a pre-packaged form to send to prospective authors, giving them enough questions that their answers will constitute a rough outline of the story.

Defining Expectations

It's also critical to let authors know ahead of time what is expected of them, and how the process will work. Pike of *Hart's E&P* explains his approach in terms of a process. "First, we delineate clearly what we expect in an article before we agree to publish it. Second, we follow up with a set of author's guidelines. Third, we review first drafts and return written comments to the authors."

Michael Ivanovich, editor of Cleveland-based *HPAC Engineering,* which covers the heating, piping, and air conditioning industries, says he helps authors by telling them what kind of article they're looking for (scope, schedule, word budget), and asking them to provide an abstract and outline before sitting down to write. "This helps us reach an agreement on the article's content before we get the first draft," he says. "It is common for authors to receive an assignment and then change it somehow. This is preferred because

GUIDELINES FOR PRODUCING A CASE HISTORY

Answers to the following questions should provide enough basic information to create a first-draft manuscript. From there, the editor can embellish the information presented, to turn a list of answers into an application story. Some questions will be more important than others, depending upon the application, but this format will generally lead to a good draft. Any additional information can be incorporated into a revised draft.

1. Briefly, what does the machine do?

2. What advantages does this machine have over its competition?

3. How does the machine operate? (For example, if it is a manually-operated machine, what tasks are required of the operator? If it is automatic, what does it do after the operator pushes a start button?)

4. What operations are accomplished by using hydraulics or pneumatics?

5. In detail, how does the hydraulic system operate? Use of schematic diagrams and descriptions of physical parameters (forces, pressures, bores, strokes, displacements, speeds, etc.) is strongly encouraged.

6. Why was fluid power chosen to control these functions instead of, say, an electromechanical system?

7. Are there any electronic controls incorporated into the fluid power system? If so, please elaborate.

8. What are the benefits of this particular design over alternative solutions? For example, longer life, higher performance, greater reliability, improved operator friendliness, easier troubleshooting, etc. Please go into as much detail as necessary.

9. When design was complete and the system tested, were there any unforeseen problems that had to be solved? Were any unexpected benefits realized that had not been anticipated? If so, please elaborate.

10. Please provide color photos of the equipment at work, if possible. (Black-and-white photos are certainly better than no photos at all.) Photos showing dirt on the machine are preferred over pretty product photos in a parking lot. Close-ups of key design features or components are also helpful. 5x7 color prints are ideal, but supply graphics in a way most convenient for you. We can even work with snapshots and sketches on napkins if necessary.

Courtesy *Hydraulics & Pneumatics*

then the author will be more enthusiastic and draw more of their personal experience and personality into the article. This is something our readers enjoy—the flavor of personality. While very technical, our articles are also usually very much alive."

To help ensure that contributors actually write something new and don't get bogged down covering things the publication has covered before, Ivanovich is working to provide authors with a CD of the magazine's past content, going back about 10 years. As the CD would be fully text-searchable, authors could do a considerable amount of research on what's been published before, helping them avoid redundancy and move the editorial content forward. The long-term goal is that future technical articles will do a better job of weaving past articles into the present, thus enriching the entire body of the publication.

"If, in the future, we can create hyperlinks that manifest references into active links, then we'll have created a phenomenal technical education and training resource for our industry," Ivanovich says.

Another assistance *HPAC Engineering* has started recently is educating its authors about the publishing business. "By informing them of how we go to market and all the variables and challenges we face in publishing a magazine, they develop more interest in the process," Ivanovich says. "We believe they will be more likely to meet deadlines, knowing what happens to us if they don't. They will also be encouraged to do a better job all the way around by becoming aware of, for example, the downstream uses and applications of their articles for education and training."

Revision and Fact Checking

Submission of the draft article is the point at which editors step in with rewriting and fact checking, but the extent to which the contributor is expected to execute changes based on the editor's comments varies by publication.

At *Hart's E&P,* the first draft is edited and corrected by the editor assigned to the article, and is subsequently proofread by the managing editor. It is then returned to the author for corrections and revisions to content only. External authors correct facts only; style and grammar edits are made by the editorial staff.

SQL Server uses a three-step process. The editor sends three versions of the article to the author for proofing and to answer questions. The first version is the primary editor's main edit and contains most of the major questions and editing comments and suggestions. The second version reflects changes that a second editor makes and any remaining questions. The last version is in two-column format, similar to how the text will appear in the magazine, and helps the author look at the content with fresh eyes. "This last version gives the author a final opportunity to make sure all changes sent in for version two were implemented by the editor and that the article is accurate," says Blomstrom.

All of *HPAC Engineering's* articles and most of its departments (those that are by-lined) are double-blind peer reviewed by two or three industry experts. "Sometimes, when the article is highly technical or gets a conflicting review (reviewers disagree with each other or the author disagrees with a reviewer), then I'll bring in an expert to arbitrate," says Ivanovich. "If the article gets extensive comments, we might have it reviewed again. In rare cases, we'll reject an article. Given the effort that goes into features, we would rather work hard to salvage an article than scuttle it after a bad review."

Given time and resource pressures on editors, having industry experts as reviewers can be key to spotting factual errors that would otherwise be missed. "We'll do our best to check references and specifications," says Ivanovich. "The key is having board members that are picky about such things, and that want you to send them the articles needing that kind of review. Matchmaking is an important part of our editorial process. This is why we have such a large board. We need two or three experts for each major industry sector we serve, and even with 40 members we are stretched thin."

The Technical Article from Scratch

Outside experts bring the industry expertise to write technical articles for trade publications, but for any number of reasons it makes sense for in-house staff to generate technical articles, and in these cases the editing issues are much the same.

Why would you use in-house writers on a topic? There are any number of reasons, but some articles are clearly best executed by staff writers. For one reason, they're positioned to write about issues and products from a perspective that can be broader than that of the industry expert, who can't be expected to treat competitive viewpoints or products objectively. In how-to features and other types of narrowly targeted articles, the absence of a broad perspective doesn't diminish the value of the information in the article. But where multiple products and viewpoints are crucial, it makes sense to use in-house staff.

Do in-house staff bring sufficient expertise to the task? In some cases, an editor on a technical magazine comes from the industry the publication serves. Some magazines find it's easier to teach an industry expert to write than it is to teach a person with a journalism degree a particular specialty. Given that the specialty may not be of interest to the journalist, the magazine may experience rapid turnover, disposing the staff to hire industry types.

Publications employing industry-bred editors tend to author more technical articles in-house, which can be a double-edged sword. Articles written by staff take more time to research and write. They require interviewing multiple sources, which are not always necessary with single-source, outside-authored pieces. In either case, the editor needs to make sure the proper balance is achieved and that the article provides value to readers.

When technical articles are staff written, whether from an industry-bred or a journalism-bred writer, interviewing multiple experts is crucial. Unlike a single-source, expert-written article in which a certain perspective from that person's industry background or research is understood, a staff-written piece is expected to be comparative. If multiple (competitive) technologies are vying for readers' attention, all of the technologies must be discussed within the article, ideally with quotes from sources that can give unbiased opinions.

E-mail makes it easier for the editor to obtain commentary from busy expert sources who can be difficult to reach. E-mail-based interviews are increasing in popularity, and in a fashion enabling editors to cast a wider net, contacting more sources than in the past. Commentary that's generated via email can be chosen based on its technical merit and objectivity. Quotes that are simply marketing ploys for a particular technology can be discarded.

Presentation

Although editors hope readers hang on their every word, most realize that that isn't always the case. Reader time constraints make it unlikely that anyone other than those with a significant professional interest in the topic will invest the time to plow through a few thousands words of technical copy.

Especially with technical articles, a visual component or graphical description is critical. Readers need multiple entry points to determine whether to invest their time in the article and, if so, how deeply into it they want to go. At the same time, editors want to provide value to readers who want to glean something from the article without investing more than a few minutes in it.

"Graphics are important for two reasons," says Pike. "First, they aid readers' understanding of the article. This is especially important with technical articles where a graphic of a process or piece of equipment may be more easily understood than several paragraphs of copy. Second, they are an important design feature of the magazine and make the difference between a visually appealing publication and one that is easy to pass over. We attempt to include at least one significant graphic per page and two where possible."

Graphics issues are covered in detail in Chapters 9 and 10, but there are a few points to be touched on here in connection with technical editing.

What to Use

The use of graphics goes beyond mere photographs. Graphics in technical features should encompass illustrations and charts to help readers digest the totality of the information being presented.

"Tables are great for providing lists and definitions," says Blomstrom. "We find that text explanations bog down when we're comparing costs, performance, percentage increases and decreases of market share, and so on. We turn to tables and graphs to convey this information quickly and visually."

The presentation of a feature from *Hydraulics & Pneumatics* showing the main hydraulic features in a commercial airliner accomplishes several reader goals:

- compresses a significant amount of data into an easy to comprehend format;
- draws readers into the article, where that much additional body text would have probably scared them off;
- reinforces what is being explained in the main article;
- allows the time-constrained reader to get the information they need quickly.

Obtaining and Selecting Graphics—Editorial Issues

Despite their importance, graphics for technical articles can be a challenge to secure and structure. Contributors may create their own charts and graphs and provide photographs to accompany their text, but it typically makes sense for editors to rebuild graphics from scratch and be selective in using supplied photographs.

"In the interest of maintaining a consistent style throughout the magazine, any figure, table, or chart that is submitted will be recreated by our in-house art director," says Halverson.

Hart's E&P sends a sheet with its author's guidelines detailing specifically the graphic quality level required. Even so, the quality of what it typically receives is mixed. "We receive substandard graphics more often than not," says Pike. "It's then a back and forth process to obtain the correct quality."

In rebuilding graphics, simplicity is key. "The information we're trying to convey is often complex, so the graphic needs to be as straightforward and self-explanatory as possible," says Blomstrom. "We try to use primary colors that are easily distinguishable from each other, and we use clear labels and legends. Many times, authors don't spend as much time on the graphics as they do on their articles, but a well-done table, chart, or drawn figure can be a key element of an article. Our editors devote a lot of time to making sure our infographics make sense and edit these elements as rigorously as they do the main article text."

Photos pose their own hurdles, in part because the interest of companies and magazines tend to diverge on what makes good editorial sense. When articles focus on particular applications, most magazines prefer to use action photos. *Hydraulics & Pneumatics* would rather show a hydraulic press on a shop floor, dirty and grimy, than a new model sitting in a parking lot. But machine manufacturers are more likely to have the glamour shot (for use in their marketing material) and tend to prefer that these photos be published.

Adding to the frustration is the fact that many smaller trade and association publications don't have the editorial budget to allow for sending a photographer to various sites. But there are steps editors can take to address this. One solution is for the editor to take photos when traveling on assignment. Many magazines work this way, and many editors have become by default staff photographers, even shooting an occasional cover shot. If a professional photographer is absolutely necessary, one cost saving move is to hire a freelance photographer in the area where the story is set. Editors can contact the local daily newspaper or find a local trade magazine through the member database of professional editor associations such as the American Society of Business Publication Editors to get a referral.

Setting Information Aside

More can be said about sidebars than can be treated here. But there are a few points to note. Sidebars add great value for readers of a technical article, presenting information that otherwise wouldn't fit well within the structure of the main text. "They can bring in an alternative viewpoint on a controversial topic, authored by someone on the other side of an issue," says Ivanovich. "They can highlight war stories or case studies without interrupting the flow of an article. Or they can establish a stand-alone entity or process (like a checklist or step-wise procedure) that will make readers want to save the article for future application."

Sidebars can also serve as less technical entry points to readers with less knowledge of the main topic, a point many editors forget as they wrestle with the main feature. Lastly, when they are properly used, they can serve to break up blocks of text, further adding to the graphical look of the feature.

Mastering the Challenge

Constructing a balanced, easy-to-digest, and useful technical article is the principal challenge of a technical trade publication editor. Making it more challenging still are the resources, or lack of them, that many editors wrestle with on a daily basis. It's not enough to do everything right in building a strong technical feature for your magazine; you must build it within the resource constraints that characterize many trade publications.

"Unfortunately, there is less time to develop and maintain the quality personal relationships our magazine needs to keep abreast of developments and to find authors and prospective board members," one editor says. "We cannot harvest the resources we developed over the past five years. We are not attending nearly enough conferences and trade shows, making enough reader calls, attending chapter meetings of associations to meet the people we need. We're becoming too reliant on existing contacts and their contacts."

Blomstrom sums up her challenges on *SQL Server:* "Trying to provide comprehensive technical information in limited space is a challenge. Authors have to assume a certain level of reader experience and knowledge. However, many authors assume too much. We like to help bridge the gaps in such articles by at least providing parenthetical definitions or short, explanatory phrases to remind readers of what a certain function does, for example, or to point readers in the right direction if they need to learn more about a concept they're unfamiliar with. These small definitions or explanations take little time or space and can give readers some quick context that helps guide them through an article they otherwise might give up on."

That said, the challenges are clearly worth it. The impact of an effective technical article is something of a gift that keeps on giving; it's a resource that technical professionals return to again and again and becomes part of the body of technical knowledge that industries rely on to grow. And therein lies the editor's satisfaction.

Concluding Information

When Jargon Works

Every trade publication editor wrestles with the use of jargon when presenting a technical article. How much jargon is too much? When is the use of jargon appropriate? Clearly, knowing the expectations of your readers is central to how you employ jargon in your publication. Here's how editorial trainer Ann Wylie of Wylie Communications approaches the jargon issue:

Does jargon ever work?

You bet it does.

For one thing, jargon makes communicating more efficient. It would be hard to communicate to professional editors, for example, if I had to define "lead" in every reference. But editors know what a lead is, so we can save a lot of words and time by using the language of our business.

The same thing is true in companies. At Domino's, the pizza delivery company was able to live up to its guarantee—"in 30 minutes or less"—because it uses jargon as a shortcut to communication.

"Domino's Pizza saves time when taking down a customer's order by using an elaborate system of symbols called the item code," writes Gwen Foss in *Maledicta,* a communications journal.

Thanks to the code, I can buy a PORSH (pepperoni, onion, black olives, sausage, and ham) and get change back from my $20. My husband can get PMS (pepperoni, mushroom, sausage).

And that's great—for insiders. But jargon never works for outsiders.

Educate or translate.

So here's how you can decide whether to use jargon in your communication:

1. Determine whether you're writing to insiders or outsiders.

2. If you're writing to insiders, EDUCATE them about your language. (After all, there's got to be a newbie at Domino's who doesn't know that BOP is beef, onion, and pepperoni.)

3. If you're writing to outsiders, TRANSLATE your language into theirs. Domino's customers, for example, need never know that an onion, red pepper, green pepper, anchovies, sausage, and mushroom pizza is really an ORGASM.

Bottom line: Don't use your insider language when communicating with outsiders.

Note: As president of Wylie Communications Inc., Ann Wylie works with communicators who want to reach more readers and with organizations that want to get the word out. To learn more about her training, consulting or writing and editing services, call Ann at 816/502-7894 or email her at awylie@WylieComm.com. Get FREE subscription to Ann's email newsletter at http://www.wyliecomm.com/newsletter.shtml.

See chapter exercise at the back of this book.

Technical Editing II

7

Tough on Facts, Easy on Words

Sylvia L. Dawson

How do you edit technical material written by subject-matter experts who know their field but don't know how to organize their material into a piece that communicates something useful to their readers?

The goal is to revise the piece, responsibly but thoroughly, without editing it out of context.

The task is an important one. I've seen many reporters from the newspaper side of journalism hired as junior editors for the business press fizzle out after a short time and return to the world of reporting because of hand-wringing over editing subject-matter experts.

The differences between technical writing and writing for a consumer audience is behind this angst. Editors must practice their craft with those differences in mind.

While it is customary in newspapers and consumer magazines for writers to target their piece to a broad audience, technical writers gear their writing to an audience that approaches the article already familiar with much of the subject and its jargon.

This is where the challenge of editing comes in, because unless editors are familiar with the industry their publication covers, they will be tempted to edit the article to suit their level of understanding, which at its most harmless can dilute the effectiveness of the article and at its most harmful can change the meaning of the original text.

The aim of the business press editor, then, is to help writers translate their knowledge into an article that effectively conveys the writer's intent without changing the writer's voice. Here's one process to follow.

Clean the Draft

First, give the original draft a quick cleaning. It's not necessary to do this yourself. If you have an assistant editor or other person on staff responsible for reviewing submitted material before it is introduced to the editing process, then this person can clean up the text for you.

The staff person can make sure the writer has met the assignment, has left no queries in the text, and has met the submission criteria (i.e., has included samples,

Sylvia L. Dawson is visiting assistant professor of journalism at Metropolitan State College, Denver.

Article courtesy of *Printwear* and *Promowear* magazines, National Business Media, Broomfield, Colo.

photographs or other artwork, etc.), as spelled out in the contributor's contract. The assistant can also proofread the draft for obvious, non-substantive errors.

Second, begin substantive editing. You handle this. As many errors as possible should be corrected during the initial stages of editing. This typically requires you to make broad organizational changes as well as narrow sentence restructurings.

Expect the writing of a subject-matter expert to be looser and less focused than what you're used to reading from journalists, so it is the job of the editor to make the writing as concise as possible.

A key objective will be learning when to leave in detail and when to leave it out. In other words, learning how to edit technical material for *word* economy and not *fact* economy. If it's clear a text needs a lot of work but you've yet to hone in on the most effective way to convey the central theme of the piece, make your task easier by simply trimming away unnecessary words. Clearing away some of the underbrush in the writing in this way helps you get a cleaner picture of what broader changes need to be done.

Take a look at the opening paragraph of a draft on natural fabrics written by an industry specialist for a trade publication covering the textile industry.

"New Directions In the Apparel Industry

Clothing, the 2nd basic human need among Food-Clothing-Shelter, continues to grow as population grows and affordability increases all over the world. Catering to this need is a vast global industry with different countries & regions specializing in some part of the production chain depending on weather, agriculture, human resources or industrial capabilities."

The text contains grammatical and style errors that can be corrected with little fuss, but their effect is insidious because they undermine your confidence that you're in the hands of a sure-footed writer. The errors put you on alert that the text will require major reorganization. That said, it might help to spend a few minutes cleaning the opening up a bit, even if it's unlikely you'll retain it in anything close to its original form. One way to clean it up would be like this:

"The demand for clothing, one of the basic human needs along with food and shelter, is growing as populations around the world increase and textiles become more affordable. Catering to this need is an apparel industry that has expanded globally as manufacturers locate pieces of their production chain in countries and regions based on their advantages in weather, agriculture, human resources, and industrial capacity."

More importantly than these grammatical and stylistic matters is the challenge of the text's direction. It's unclear where the writer is going, although we assume it will have something to do with the cost-effective manufacture of textiles. Here's the second paragraph of the original draft:

"The growth in production of clothing has led to concerns about the depletion of resources & the effects on the environment due to the waste generated. Due to consumer demands, there is a renewed interest in natural products & revisiting of some of the oldest fabric sources known to humans. All of these can be put under one category—vegetable fibers. Each material has unique characteristics that make it desirable for use."

We see something of the piece's direction here. A negative by-product of the global textile industry's success in affordably meeting the demands of a growing population is environmental stress, and there's a way to address this stress while still meeting our clothing needs: a return to vegetable fibers in textile selection. Then we read the third paragraph:

"The Ad Specialty Industry though smaller compared to the broader Apparel Industry, is subject to the same consumer demands with a bit of delay & can benefit by looking into similar products as the trend develops."

We now hear about a certain part of the apparel industry, referred to as the ad specialty industry (promotional products distributors), and that this part of the industry would do well to look into the use of vegetable fibers. This theme is developed a bit more in the fourth paragraph:

"The apparel industry always experiments with new materials or design, some of which find wider acceptance & long term usage. The Ad-specialty industry seems to follow the more accepted developments. The interest in new products is very strong in the boutiques & catalog/web based companies serving niche markets. The ASI industry having a similar niche focus can benefit from this strength. Some suppliers have started to offer these products as they may offer specific solutions to the different segments in the ad specialty industry."

The direction of the piece is fairly clear now, so the task of the editor is to reconstruct the opening to take the guesswork out of the draft. That will require reconstructing the piece. The style and grammar problems essentially become moot.

One way to reconstruct the piece is as we've done below. Of course, there are other ways to do it and still remain faithful to the voice of the writer and the aim of the text. The way we approach it here makes it clear in the first few sentences where the writer is going with the piece. The reconstructed version follows the original draft.

A couple of quick notes before we get to the text:

Jargon.   Early in the original draft the writer mentions the "Ad Specialty Industry" without explaining what that term means. It's safe to say the readers of *Promowear,* one of the target magazines of the piece, come to the text familiar with the term. But specialty references such as that one should be defined, at least on first reference, so the text doesn't contain mysteries to readers not familiar with every term. In the edited version "Ad Specialty Industry" is replaced with the self-defining "promotional products distributors." Now every reader can follow along without stumbling over the undefined term.

The four Cs: *correct, concise, consistent, and complete.*   Don't neglect to verify the proper names, and their spelling, of people, places, and that all verifiable facts are confirmed, and all numbers (statistics, tables, charts) accurate. Review the piece in its entirety to be sure it's as tightly written as possible. Also check references for consistency. Don't talk about the "Internet" in one sentence and the "internet" in another. Stick with your preferred style manual—*The AP Stylebook* and *Libel Manual* or *The Chicago Manual of Style*—without exception. Make sure the story is complete—the who, what, where, why, and when have been answered—by rereading after you've completed editing.

Communication with writer.   If you have questions, ask—especially when the text is heavy on technical jargon. Whatever your policy on the changes outside authors can make once the draft is edited, in some instances you'll need to get their input into your changes. Make sure the article hasn't been edited out of context. It's safe to say that many contributors will ask you to make them "look good" in print and will appreciate the opportunity to see their edited product before it is published. Often, they will only suggest minor changes and help you clarify details they may have not clearly communicated or that may have been obscured during the editing process.

Practice.   The beauty of editing is the more you do it, the more proficient you will become, and style errors that used to slip by will soon be jumping out at you. The key is to learn the ins-and-outs of your industry, know your stylebook, and practice. Then you'll be able to edit material for any publication with confidence.

■ ■ ■

Original Draft

New Directions In the Apparel Industry

Clothing, the 2nd basic human need among Food-Clothing-Shelter, continues to grow as population grows and affordability increases all over the world. Catering to this need is a vast global industry with different countries & regions specializing in some part of the production chain depending on weather, agriculture, human resources or industrial capabilities.

The growth in production of clothing has led to concerns about the depletion of resources & the effects on the environment due to the waste generated. Due to consumer demands, there is a renewed interest in natural products & revisiting of some of the oldest fabric sources known to humans. All of these can be put under one category—vegetable fibers. Each material has unique characteristics that make it desirable for use.

The Ad Specialty Industry though smaller compared to the broader Apparel Industry, is subject to the same consumer demands with a bit of delay & can benefit by looking into similar products as the trend develops.

The apparel industry always experiments with new materials or design, some of which find wider acceptance & long term usage. The Ad-specialty industry seems to follow the more accepted developments. The interest in new products is very strong in the boutiques & catalog/web based companies serving niche markets. The ASI industry having a similar niche focus can benefit from this strength. Some suppliers have started to offer these products as they may offer specific solutions to the different segments in the ad specialty industry.

Although each natural material has some very strong desirable characteristics, they have some limitations in their natural form in delivering what is needed to meet the demands of modern times. Of all the natural fibers, cotton gained most acceptability in the manufacture of apparel, while the other vegetable fibers were sidestepped or remained only in industrial uses until recently.

The limitations *[all of which are not shared by all fibers]* in general which made natural fibers fall out of grace are:

Coarseness or unevenness of the fibers, making weaving a difficult process.

Difficult & cumbersome Manufacturing process,

Brittleness—in most cases—which wears & breaks the fibers with creasing, sharp folds in the same areas & wrinkles easily.

Poor elasticity & resilience—do not spring back to original shape & size easily

Price—some natural fibers were expensive to produce & were replaced by synthetic materials or other natural fibers or blends.

Natural fibers & their use in making fabrics are believed to have been known for at least 10,000 years. There are many natural fibers that are known, which were in use before or are being used today for apparel or industrial purposes.

Among these cotton comes from the flower of a plant while vegetable fibers from the bast [thin layer of fibers growing between the bark & the stalk] of a plant. Among the many natural fibers, the following were more widely used in different regions of the world.

Cotton	Linen/Flax	Ramie	Soy based fibers	Mescal
Silk	Hemp	Jute	Coconut	Sisal

Materials made from natural fibers like Linen, Ramie & Hemp have been discovered in tombs & pyramids dating back to 8,000 B.C. For thousands of years natural fibers like hemp was put to industrial uses. Sailors relied upon hemp cordage for strength to hold their ships and sails, and the coarseness of the fiber made it useful for canvas, sailcloth, sacks, rope, and paper. In fact, its combination of ruggedness and comfort were utilized by Levi Strauss as a lightweight duck canvas for the very first pair of jeans made in California.

Christopher Columbus & subsequent sailors crossed the oceans to America on ships rigged with hemp ropes & sails. Hemp was grown extensively in colonial America by numerous farmers including George Washington and Thomas Jefferson. Apparently, the Declaration of Independence was drafted on hemp paper & Betsy Ross sewed the first American flag from hemp.

There will be a series of special features in the following issues on the specific history & development of some of these natural fibers which are of relevance to the industry today.

With the rise of environmental consciousness & numerous improvements in technology there has been a renewal of interest in using natural fibers for their inherent eco-friendly qualities. The shortcomings of the natural fibers are being overcome by technical processes, blending with synthetics or with other natural fibers, additives in dyeing & finishing etc.

Cotton replaced many of the vegetable fibers and became the most widely used material due to ease of production & versatility. However, in the mid 20th century man made polymer based products started to replace cotton as brand new wonder materials, until the direct effects on the user & the by-products on the environment started to become apparent.

Vegetable fibers are renewable resources, need very little fertilizers or pesticides to grow and in fact can help rejuvenate the earth as a good rotation crop. They grow fast & the yield per acre in vegetable fibers is even higher than cotton in general. However, just being natural fibers does not make it environmentally sound. The process by which these fibers are converted into fabrics is very important, especially when produced in a mass industrial scale. The dyes that are used for color, the finishes for special effects & the washes that the garment goes through is important in achieving the goal of maintenance & repair of the environment.

- In addition to the desirable environmental qualities, natural fibers also are endearing for several functional reasons:
- Breathable, absorbent & quick drying: They breathe much better than synthetics & absorb moisture away from the body to make them feel comfortable & cooler to the body.
- Fiber strength & durability—very strong fibers—silk is supposed to be more strong than steel for the same thickness of filament. These are durable & abrasion resistant even in high heat & moisture conditions.
- Character: Designers after ceasing to marvel at the uniformity & evenness of manmade fibers for decades are turning to natural fibers due to the lack of uniformity & hence a unique character presented by fabrics made from these fibers.
- Luster: These fibers possess a Natural luster which is elegant & usually gets better with usage & washes. Linen & silk need no introduction as to the desirable qualities of natural materials.
- Bio-degradable: This feature is important for environmental reasons as well as for use in some civil engg/industrial uses where it is important that the fabric bond with the surroundings with time.

Hydrocarbon free: Some natural fibers like jute, is used for bags for packing coffee, cocoa, peanut, or other food grain where it is important to avoid contamination by hydrocarbon & kersenic smell.

The future of natural fibers is very encouraging as consumers demand more sensitivity to the environment & human use of industrially processed materials. Consumer demand is going to be the factor driving industries to explore, find better materials & technology.

The use of new technologies to overcome the shortcomings of specific natural fibers & blending of synthetic and natural fibers or different kinds of natural fibers seems to be an increasing trend in the future of apparel industry.

■ ■ ■

EDITED VERSION

New Directions in the Apparel Industry

Natural Fibers: The Eco-Friendly Alternative

The apparel industry is changing, growing. And along with this growth has come concern about the depletion of global resources, as well as the environmental effects of wastes generated as a by-product of apparel manufacturing. These concerns, while not particularly new to the industry, have increased consumer demand for natural and environmentally responsible fabrics.

Due to this increased interest in natural products, many manufacturers are revisiting some of the oldest fabric sources known to man—vegetable fibers. Each of these "rediscovered" materials has unique characteristics that make it desirable for use in the production of apparel, and each offers unique sales opportunities for promotional-products distributors. Although promotional apparel represents just a portion of the broad apparel industry, distributors can surely benefit by closely observing these trends and reacting appropriately to the opportunities they provide.

The process of experimenting with new materials is commonplace in the apparel industry. While some experimentation leads to little in the way of staying power and popularity, some receive great acceptance and long-term success, depending on the product's inherent strengths and weaknesses as an apparel fabrication. And natural fibers, it goes without saying, are among the eternal fabric favorites.

Natural Fit

The practice of utilizing natural fibers for the purpose of making fabrics is believed to be approximately 10,000 years old. Because of that extended history, there are numerous natural fibers available for garment manufacturing.

Along with the numerous recent improvements in manufacturing technology, there has also been a renewal of interest in natural fibers for the inherent eco-friendly qualities and image they possess. In the past, however, the use of many of these natural fibers has been limited by the shortcomings of the fibers themselves. Recent technological advances are gradually eliminating such limitations by blending the fibers with synthetics or with other complimentary natural fibers. With these limitations coming under control, modern apparel manufacturers can focus on the positive aspects of these products—and there are *many* advantages to them when used correctly.

To begin, vegetable fibers are renewable resources, meaning they grow back from season to season. Some of these fibers need very little fertilizer or pesticide to grow, and can help *rejuvenate* the earth when utilized as a rotation crop. These crops grow fast and the yield-per-acre from other vegetable fibers is generally even higher than, for example, cotton.

It is important to keep in mind that just because a fiber is natural does not necessarily mean its use is environmentally sound. The process by which these fibers are converted into fabric is very important, especially when produced on a massive industrial scale. Also, the dyes used to color the products, finishes for special effects, and the washes garments go through all contribute to the goal of maintenance and repair of the environment. But lest you think the only benefits of these products are related to the environment, it is important to note that natural fibers are endearing for several functional reasons, including

- *Breathability, absorbency and rapid-drying properties:* These products generally breathe much better than synthetics and absorb moisture away from the body, which produces garments that are comfortable and cooler to wear in heat and humidity.
- *Fiber strength and durability:* Natural fibers are quite strong. Silk is said to be stronger than steel for the same thickness of filament. Products made with natural fibers are durable and abrasion resistant, even in high heat and moisture-rich conditions.
- *Character:* Designers, after loosing interest in the uniformity and evenness of synthetic fibers, are turning to natural fibers due to their *lack* of uniformity. The variation offered by these fibers lends uniqueness and character to fabric.
- *Luster:* Many of these fibers possess a natural luster that is elegant and usually improves with wear and washing. Linen and silk need no explanation when it comes to such desirable qualities.
- *Biodegradable:* This feature is important for environmental reasons, as well as for use in some civil/industrial applications where it is important that the fabric bond with surroundings over time.
- *Hydrocarbon-free:* Some natural fibers, such as jute, are commonly used in bags for packing coffee, cocoa, peanuts and other food products with which it is important to avoid contamination by hydrocarbons.

Natural Limitations

Although each natural material has very desirable characteristics, each also has limitations in its natural form when considered in the context of the demands of modern apparel manufacturing. Of all the natural fibers, cotton has been the most strongly embraced for the manufacture of apparel, while many others have been sidestepped altogether or utilized only for obscure, peripheral industrial purposes.

Among the limitations that have contributed to some natural fibers' eventual fall from grace are a number of properties that create a challenge for garment manufacturers:

Coarseness or unevenness of fibers, which makes weaving a difficult process;

Brittleness causes easy wrinkling that, in addition to unsightliness, wears and breaks the fibers at creases and folds in laundering;

Poor elasticity and resilience causes the fabric to resist returning to its original shape and size;

Price—some natural fibers were expensive to produce and were replaced by synthetic materials, other natural fibers or blends.

Popularity Contest

Materials made from natural fibers such as linen, ramie, and hemp have been discovered in tombs and pyramids dating back to 8000 B.C. For thousands of years, natural fibers, such as hemp have been utilized in a variety of industrial applications. Sailors relied upon hemp cordage for its strength to secure ships and sails, and the coarseness of the fiber made it useful for canvas, sailcloth, sacks, rope, and paper. Christopher Columbus and subsequent sailors sailed to the New World on ships rigged with hemp ropes and sails. And the product was grown extensively in colonial America by numerous founding fathers, including George Washington and Thomas Jefferson. In fact, the Declaration of Independence was drafted on paper made of hemp, and Betsy Ross sewed the first American flag from hempen fabric. More recently— although still an historical reference from a contemporary standpoint—hemp's combination of ruggedness and comfort were employed by Levi Strauss & Co. as a lightweight duck canvas for the very first pair of jeans made in California.

The Future

The future of natural fibers is very encouraging as consumers become more aware of the environment and of human usage of industrially processed materials. Two things are certain:

Consumer demand is the driving factor in motivating industries to explore (and develop) better materials and technologies in coming years; and

The use of new technologies to overcome the shortcomings of specific natural fibers—along with the blending of such fibers with synthetics and other natural fibers— seems to be an interesting and opportunity-packed trend facing the apparel industry.

You will learn more about the specific history and course of development related to many other natural fibers in a series of special features in upcoming issues of *Promowear*. So, stay tuned.

See chapter exercise at the back of this book.

How-to Articles

8

Value Worth Tearing Out

⌐Kimberly Sweet

Editors aim to make their trade publications central to their readers' professional success, but the extent to which they succeed in that ambition depends in large measure on how well they handle how-to articles. More than any other content, how-to articles are a way of providing information that readers take away from the publication and apply directly to their work. Indeed, they're the pieces readers literally tear out and refer to again and again. How do you make your how-to articles stand out as indispensable content for your readers?

Start with the idea of show and tell, although not necessarily in that order.

In *Control Engineering,* a technology publication for engineers in the global control, instrumentation, and automation marketplace, the May 2002 cover story sought to help readers convince their managers of the benefits of installing a fieldbus network, a process control system.

The article outlined the communication problems engineers would likely face in recommending fieldbus to their managers, then suggested which advantages would be most persuasive to managers and how best to argue them. Editors were *telling* their readers the who, what, why, where, and when.

Then it switched gears and *showed* readers the how. Using case studies, it showed how 1) Rütgers Organics Corp. saved $25,000 and reduced processing time by 12-14 hours; 2) Calcasieu Refining Co. completed a control retrofit in six weeks instead of six months; and 3) OEM, AEC Corp. reduced equipment installation time by 50 percent.

Those kinds of bottom-line figures, pulled from concrete examples, are the data engineers need to take back to their corporate managers to make their case.

In the piece, which won an ASBPE 2002 national gold award for how-to articles, the two components—the show and the tell—create a compelling whole. *Telling* readers the who, what, why, where, and when set the context and *showing* readers the how made it concrete.

Clearly, effective how-to articles differ widely in approach, but they share the common elements of showing and telling.

Building your how-to content around this idea sounds easy enough. In practice, how do you get there?

Kimberly Sweet is editor of Professional Remodeler, *a Reed Business Information publication. Sweet is a graduate of the Medill School of Journalism at Northwestern University.*

Show how to do it. Helpful how-to information should stand on its own. Separating how-to information from core text enables readers to refer quickly to key information. In a solid how-to article, it's hard to break out too much information.

Before you write, picture your approach from both a content and a presentation standpoint. You must look at the two together. More than with other content in a publication, how-to articles require planning content and presentation together as a whole. Think of the last instruction manual you read. Maybe it was on how to set up a DVD player. What helped you the most—the pictures or the words or the two working together? What other elements were included? A checklist? Numbered steps? Diagrams? Glossary? List of common problems? Resources for more information?

If you include these elements in some measure in your own work, you have a recipe for an effective how-to article.

Here's a brief look at a few of the elements that work best when content and presentation are conceived together, and the showing and the telling are paired at the outset of planning.

Text and Graphics

Think about how to deploy photos, illustrations, charts, and other graphic elements to convey the information more effectively than words alone can. Your art

Let sidebars do the talking. Checklists, graphics, photos, lists of key facts, and other information break-outs reinforce the core message in the text. Reproduction of original source material can be effective, too. With how-tos, the focus should be on *showing*. And don't forget to provide plenty of resources for readers to get more information on their own.

director, if brought in at the beginning of planning, can help here. But planning a how-to presentation is very much an editorial function, and should be led by editorial needs.

In a piece on time management and productivity, the May/June 2003 issue of *Success in Home Care* chronicled a day in the life of a nurse. The piece told the who, what, why, where, and when of a typical day of a home healthcare nurse, then depicted a page from the nurse's day planner as a graphic image to show how the nurse managed time and productivity. The writer keyed the content off the graphic image of the day planner to document a nurse's principal tasks. Yellow blocks simulating Post-It Notes served as a visual cue for especially important information.

Plainer graphics may be just as useful. In a retirement planning story in the June 2002 issue of *Professional Remodeler,* the publication I edit, we used a simple table to highlight the differences between the main plan options. The body of the story went into detail about each one, but to compare all five against each other in text would have required more words than remodelers typically have time to read. The solution was a simple table that enabled readers to determine which type of plan was most likely to serve their companies, and enabled them to read just about that type of plan.

Importantly, the chart becomes a resource that readers can tear out and refer to later. Giving readers a tool they can take away from the magazine is one of the key objectives of a trade publication editor.

In the time management piece in *Success in Home Care,* editors created a blank daily activity log that readers could photocopy for their own use or use as a template for creating their own log. Note. *Success in Home Care* created the log based on what actually works for people who are successful in their profession. Although the editors could have provided a daily activity log based on their own knowledge of the industry, the log's usefulness and credibility are enhanced by the credibility of its source.

Checklists and At-a-Glance Boxes

In your effort to save your readers' time without sacrificing the value of the information you're providing, it's helpful to employ small graphic devices such as checklists and boxes that support your content.

Checklists are relied on to list important facts about a subject, such as the steps of, or the items used in, a procedure. At-a-glance boxes offer an overview in a small sidebar. In a profile, an at-a-glance box might offer some of the highlights of an individual's career, but in a how-to article, an at-a-glance box provides something more concrete such as the key features of a device in short format.

An at-a-glance box can help in spurring a reader's recall of the article, too. It's a visual clue to the article contents, helping the reader to recall the important information it contained. Or, if some readers don't have time to read the article in the first place, it gives them the key points so that they can take away value from the information.

Both checklists and at-a-glance lists offer entry points into the material, help simplify complex content, and make the information in a how-to article more usable. Depending on their content, the devices might be located near the relevant portion of the text or at the beginning of a story, to explain what's to come.

In its piece on the fieldbus network, *Control Engineering* employed two checklists, one noting what an engineer must do to justify a fieldbus network, the other noting what users must *show* or prove. The crucial challenges and solutions are distilled to their most basic essence.

Computerworld used a similar strategy in a May 10, 2002 piece looking at differences between two major platforms. It summed up the crux of the matter with a pro-and-con chart. The body of the article walked readers through the decision-making process and the questions they needed to ask themselves, but the most essential information was encapsulated in an easy-to-read, easy-to-remember format.

The retirement planning piece in *Professional Remodeler* included a snapshot box of key aspects of one remodeler's business (number of employees, annual sales, etc.) to help readers decide how closely this company resembled their own, and therefore whether the retirement plan included in the case study would work for them.

Other information set off on its own included details on the annual administration cost of the plan selected in the case study.

Resource List

Despite our best efforts to make every word count, no piece can cover the breadth and depth of a topic. So don't try! Your readers will thank you. If they wanted to read a book on the topic, they would. Stick to one angle; the rest of the info can go in a bibliography.

But don't just give readers a starting point for more information. Give them ideas on how to *act*. Help them get started. Web sites, e-mail addresses, and phone numbers should be included for readers who want to act on what they've read right away. In a June 2002 piece on implementing information technology in the classroom, *Technology & Learning* gave readers names and contact information for three major types of technology products and services directed at educators. That's information that readers could act on right then and there.

Numbered Steps

Use numbers to lead readers through a step-by-step guide. In the *Technology & Learning* piece, readers are led through four broad steps for setting up information management systems. The numbers of each step are treated as a graphic image to help break up the page, with bold intros helping to set apart each question to be asked under each step. A glossary placed near step one ensures readers can easily access explanation of terms likely to be unfamiliar.

Taking the How-to Online

How-to articles lend themselves to infinite possibilities on the Internet, which can accommodate text, graphics, photos, and illustrations to an extent that print publications typically can't. As a resource, a Web publication associated with your print publication can expand your options tremendously. A Web publication also gives you a vehicle for adding content of a type that you can't use in a print publication such as video clips and databases.

What material should you post on your publication's Web site? Start with material gathered during the reporting process. For its piece on the fieldbus network, *Control Engineering* posted an expanded version of the article and longer versions of each of its case studies. In a typical case at *Professional Remodeler,* we post photographs that build on the content in the print publication, including additional photos showing the construction phase of a project from a variety of angles. These additional photos aren't just nice to have; they give readers more help in visualizing a complicated procedure.

Another option is to upload any forms, templates, spreadsheets, etc., referred to in a print story. In 2001, *Professional Remodeler* featured a year-long how-to series called "Blueprint for Success" that covered the nine key areas of business expertise for a remodeling company. With each installment, the editors included relevant tools either in print or online. The Worksheets section of the Web site, where the forms and other resources such as blueprints are kept, has become one of the top-ranked sections of the site, as determined by hits.

Note: It goes without saying that the danger in posting material on the Web lies in forgetting that we are editors, and it's our job to gather, sort, and analyze information for our readers. Sometimes sidebars or pictures weren't cut from the print publication for lack of space but because they didn't add to the story or their quality didn't meet publication standards. Turning your Web site into a final resting place for purple prose will not endear you to your audience.

Concluding Information

How to Avoid Getting Sued

Accuracy is the bottom line for all journalism, but it can take on heightened importance with a how-to article, given its aim to offer guidance for action. Clearly, as an editor you need to be scrupulous in the soundness of the information you publish.

For *Professional Remodeler,* the publication I edit, household mold provides a textbook case of why scrupulousness in the quality of your information is so crucial.

Anyone who picked up a newspaper or watched television news in 2002 heard about mold and the concerns it raises for one's house and health. They may have also heard about the spread of lawsuits against homebuilders. Armed with information they received in consumer media, homeowners filed a rash of lawsuits accusing builders of using construction practices or building products that encouraged mold growth.

In this environment, journalists in the homebuilding and remodeling industries know that any how-to construction article that touched on practices that could be alleged to cause mold could end up as evidence in a lawsuit. The situation is complicated by the fact that building practices differ by climate and installation techniques differ by product. Yet, avoiding the topic wasn't an option. A how-to on implementing building practices that prevent mold was among the most valuable information editors could provide in this environment. Yet it was also potentially dangerous to us.

Each industry and profession has sensitive issues similar to this one in the construction trades. To navigate this environment, take a few steps beyond the usual care for accurate reporting:

- If the topic is highly technical, enlist an expert to write the technical portions if not the entire piece.
- Before publication, run the story by an editorial advisory board, if you have one, and otherwise be sure to seek input from industry professionals who represent a range of expertise. They'll see the issues from different angles.
- Enlist your company's legal counsel, if it has one, to review the piece before publication.
- Give your publisher a heads-up. This won't keep you from getting sued if there's a problem, but it could keep you from losing your job!

Visual Design I

9

Telling the Story, Showing the Benefit

Mary Boltz Chapman

Words and pictures work together. But how they work together for a consumer audience isn't necessarily the same as how they work together for a professional audience.

To be sure, there are publication design rules that make sense, no matter what kind of publication you're editing. Serif fonts tend to be easier to read on the printed page than sans serif fonts, for example, so consumer and trade publications alike tend to use serif fonts for their main body type. In a similar manner, type arranged into shapes such as circles and triangles is hard to read, so publications tend to avoid such fancy treatments—or at least they should.

That said, trade and consumer publications are different. The aim of trade publications is to help their readers in their jobs, and everything about the design should be in the service of that aim. Although it is important for consumer publications to help readers, they also seek to entertain and to merely inform.

Given trade publications' focus on service journalism, thinking visually for editors means thinking of ways to use design as an instrument for helping readers take something of value away from the publication.

Think about how readers use your publication's information. In the publication I edit, *Chain Leader,* a monthly magazine for restaurant company executives, we run a feature called "Restauratour." In this feature, we present a photo tour of a new or updated chain restaurant. Restaurant executives take ideas away from the feature for use in their own companies. To show even more than the pictures alone can, we run a floor plan of the restaurant, indicating where and from what angle each picture was taken. The photo tour, in combination with the floor plan, is a use of design that enhances the take-away value for readers.

Likewise, we do a monthly "Storyboard" article that discusses a restaurant chain's advertising campaign. Consumers see commercials on TV. Those creating them see them on storyboards. So we set up the images to look like a storyboard, complete with

Mary Boltz Chapman, a foodservice journalist for more than a dozen years, is editor-in-chief, Chain Leader, *a monthly magazine for senior executives of restaurant companies published by Reed Business Information. Mary holds a degree in journalism from the College of St. Francis.*

Think in visual mode.
Words are only half the tools
available to trade publication
editors as they strive to present information in a way that
helps readers in their jobs.
Pictures are the other half.
Think in visual terms from
the beginning of your story
planning process. Doing so
helps keep you and the designer on the same page as
you start moving the story
from an idea to a visual presentation.

Used with permission from
Chain Leader, copyright © Reed
Business Information, a division
of Reed Elsevier Inc.; photography by Kingmond Young.

Sophisticated elements such
as darker wood and wrought
iron distinguish Olive
Garden's Chelsea restaurant
from the chain's "Tuscan
Farmhouse" prototype.

The urban unit's foyer and
waiting area (opposite) are
bigger than most Manhattan
restaurants.

BRIGHT LIGHTS
BIG GARDEN

*Olive Garden designs a sleek, but not small,
prototype for dense urban locales.*

BY LISA BERTAGNOLI

captions. Thus, our readers take away examples that they can use as they create their
own TV advertising plans.

For our advertising index, which we call "Vendor Exchange," we found that our
readers did not use any of the feedback mechanisms we have tested, which include
bingo cards and fax-back forms. So we simply supply the phone numbers and Internet addresses for each advertiser, with a brief description of their product or service.
To make it easy to use, we organize it by type of product or service and use prominent
subheads. It's a small change, but it shows how design can be tweaked in the service
of reader usability.

Some technical publications are thought of as being similar to a boring textbook.
If you design your publication with an eye toward helping your readers, it doesn't
have to be that way. The editors of *Consulting-Specifying Engineer,* a magazine for
building engineers, revamped their publication's design to be fresh, but also to be

Used with permission from Chain Leader, copyright © Reed Business Information, a division of Reed Elsevier Inc.; photography by Kingmond Young.

Communicating with pictures. Save text for development of the article's core message, and let other types of communication—photos, graphics, diagramming—do the heavy lifting on the details. Here, interior photos flesh out a reproduction of a restaurant floor plan, giving a readership of restaurant executives a clear picture of how one restaurant is managing a challenging room layout.

more useful. Key was getting their readers on board. Now the magazine is livelier and more visual, but it's also more scannable, which means readers can take away valuable information without having to plod through heavy text.

With the idea of reader usability as our starting point, what's key for editors in guiding their publication's design? Here's my take on what the issues are, based on what I've learned as managing editor and then editor-in-chief of *Chain Leader*.

Working Together

Behind every successful trade publication is the relationship between the editor and the art director. Everything flows from that. The two of you must work to understand each other and, putting your egos aside, combine your expertise to benefit the whole. It's the art director who must translate the editorial focus, which is to help your reader, into visual reality. Thus, the art director must understand the content and the aim of that content or risk hindering the publication's ability to reach its goal.

Learn Each Other's Jargon

I began my career as a production editor, a type of liaison between the art and editorial departments, so learning both vocabularies was necessary for me. But there are editors who don't know what a serif is. There's a glossary of design terms on page 99 to help you speak the same language as your art director.

Make the Art Director Part of the Team

Art directors aren't support staff. Invite them to meetings, lunches, and celebrations. They will then feel ownership of the product and want to contribute to its success.

Communicate

Good communication will improve the way design issues are addressed. Editors may say, "This page needs something," which is too vague to be helpful. On the other hand, if you're too prescriptive—"Give me line art of a telephone"—you'll take the creativity out of the designer's hands. It helps to present the problem, but not your idea of the solution, as clearly as possible. You might say, "This page looks gray. What can we do to break it up and give readers additional take-away value?"

Allow Tweaking

Enable art directors to work with the design after the article is completed. They can tweak bad breaks; adjust those few lines you have to cut or add; and place pictures, graphs, and charts with appropriate editorial.

Reality check: In some publishing companies, there is a separate art staff, each member working on several books. Sometimes magazines see a revolving door of designers as they get shuffled and reshuffled. Artists might be hesitant to make the product their own or put any real creative effort behind their work. Or several artists put their stamp on a publication, and it turns into a hodgepodge of different styles. This is frustrating because editors and art directors are unable to build the communication necessary to put together a cohesive package. In such cases, it's necessary for the editor to be as clear as possible in communicating the focus and meaning of each story, and make sure the designers know which parameters are flexible and which are not. Designers must accept and follow the editor's direction until they know the book well enough to break the rules.

Mission

Design that serves your readers starts with your editorial mission statement. If your publication doesn't have one, or if the existing mission statement is outdated, write one. Having a mission enables everyone on staff, including the artist, to row in the same direction. The editor doesn't need to always be available to answer questions about what should go where, etc. Designers will do the right thing instead of following a set of instructions.

In developing a mission statement, define the publication's content, structure, and growth plans. Determine what sets it apart from the competition, its purpose, and the image you're trying to project. (For details on writing a mission statement, see Chapter 4 on redesigning a publication.)

Then, approach your design with an eye toward fulfilling that mission.

Communication and Planning

Frequent meetings will ensure everyone stays on the same page. It takes a lot of discipline and time we often think we don't have. In the same way you determine a magazine's mission, you need to decide on and communicate each story's purpose. The art director must know what the editor is trying to get across.

In *Chain Leader,* we do such planning informally, but we have the luxury of sitting in close proximity to each other. As stories are assigned, we talk about what we're trying to achieve with each. Then the art director can move forward on photo shoots or securing other art elements.

Communication between the editor and the art director enables both to have time to think creatively within the parameters of the piece's objective, and, guided by the mission statement, without having to reinvent the wheel each time.

This raises a point that in an ideal world wouldn't need mentioning. The art director can't rely on you to explain what the piece is trying to do; the art director must read the magazine.

Reality check: It is often the case that design work starts before the article is completed. In these cases, the objective of the piece must be communicated early. And the designer must have the freedom and flexibility to adjust the design, even replace it with something else, if necessary.

Simplicity and Consistency

In design, keep it simple and keep it steady over time. Using a consistent grid, white space, and type treatment adds to the publication's unity. Keeping to regular parameters reinforces the brand and helps in communication.

In *Chain Leader,* all the departments have the same treatment; the columns have the same design. We use only a few font families throughout the book, even on features.

We also keep departments and regular features in the same place, issue to issue. If readers know where to find information, they'll use the book, even if time is restricted. The goal is to be more useful to the reader. The added bonus is improved readership and loyalty.

Simple, consistent design also helps to distinguish the editorial pages from the ads. Though some advertisers try to mimic the editorial, many want their ads to stand out.

Interestingly, in cases where ads are highly visual and full bleed, editorial pages that are gray and have a lot of white space actually help make the editorial stand out. Such an idea is counterintuitive. But consider the news sections in many magazines. Advertisers like to be in the front of the book on the right hand page. Consistently gray editorial pages in those sections would stand out. Late breaking news rarely allows you time to secure good art anyway.

The more regular and simple a design is, the easier it is to execute. You can create templates, especially for different sections of the magazine, that are flexible enough for creativity but without heavy design work.

Design exceptions then have even greater impact. But use such exceptions sparingly. In any case, they require more planning and work, and who has time for more work?

Typography

Typography is a main component of design. Copy should be legible and easy to read and to scan. If it communicates easily, the story is more usable.

Type not only should aid readability; it should be appropriate to the message. The wrong type can hinder a message. It should attract the target audience, emphasize important information, and help create recognition.

Chain Leader uses three font families almost exclusively. The familiar fonts further distinguish and maintain the editorial brand. At the same time, there is enough flexibility within those families to be visually interesting.

Readability is key: it is easier to read lowercase type than all caps. It's hard to read long columns of copy. An old standard is that the ideal line width for any type is one and a half times its lowercase alphabet. Minimum width is one time; maximum is two times the alphabet.

Being creative with type can be tricky, especially if you work outside the norm. For example, depending on your printer, running colored type or copy reversed out of a photo—or a block of color other than black—can be dangerous. A tiny registration problem can make the text unreadable. If reversing type, use a larger size or bolder face. And avoid thin serifs. They tend to look even thinner.

In narrow columns of justified copy, spaces are inserted to fill up space between words and sometimes even letters, causing bad breaks and ugly gaps.

Fonts from different printers and sources look different. And in Quark, for example, the true italic or bold font might not be available—only Quark's manipulation of the Roman font. What you see on your screen might not be what you get when it's printed.

Avoid gimmicks. Text set in shapes such as circles or pyramids is a gimmick. Designers didn't do it in the old days, presumably because it was too much work and too expensive to set the type. Now it's easy to do. But use it sparingly if at all. It's cute, but how many trade magazine readers appreciate cute? Unless it's serving a purpose, it's just window dressing.

Graphics

Like bad typography, misused graphics do more harm than good. It's better to use no graphic than one that confuses the reader or muddies the point. Meaningless art means, or at least looks like, shallow content, and readers don't have time for that. Properly used graphics improve readability, clarify and explain, attract attention, and even entertain—which can be an aid in service journalism.

A good picture is one that communicates. It's not necessarily the best framed or the most focused. It's tempting to lead with the story that has the best art, or use the best photo as the hero shot, or the most prominent on the page. But since the goal is communication, the best picture is the one that reinforces the editorial.

Reality check: We have situations in which the photos that arrive are very different from what we expected. For example, the chain restaurant executives we profile are generally shot in one of their restaurants. In one case, we had to shoot the subject of the story in her office due to her busy schedule. Instead of a typical *Chain Leader* environmental portrait, we got a photograph appropriate for *Fortune*—an executive sitting on a chair in a stark office lobby. We quickly refocused the lead and changed the headline to "Sitting Tight." It wouldn't have worked if both the artist and editorial staff weren't working for the same solution.

They see themselves in that chair. A trade publication and its readers form a discrete community. The publication articles are written about the readers, for the readers, and, in some cases, by the readers. So, don't stint on putting pictures of your readers in the publication. It draws them in, and a well-thought-out photo, such as the one presented here, can communicate a lot about the tone of the article and the nature of the industry challenge it discusses.

Used with permission from *Chain Leader,* copyright © Reed Business Information, a division of Reed Elsevier Inc., photography by Mark Robert Halper.

With the technology we use today, art directors can be creative when dealing with photography: crop a picture in an extreme close-up; run it in black and white; use Sepia tones; or blur part of the image to show action. Like other tricks, don't overdo them.

If you know how pictures can be manipulated (cropped differently, color fixed, "opened up" to take out some of the black, etc.), you'll be less likely to reject them, giving the art director more images to choose from.

The ability to manipulate photos can lead to the temptation to remove wrinkles, yellow teeth, or any other flaw from head shots. Unless you work for a glossy consumer book, it probably isn't necessary. And it takes away from the person you're depicting. *Chain Leader* has a head shot of a chain executive on every cover. We limit ourselves to softening wrinkles and smoothing out skin tones.

Shadows have long been a good tool for helping make pictures jump off a page. But multiple shadows don't make sense, especially in different colors. If you're going to use shadows, make sure they all go in the same direction. If one goes down and to the right, they all should. Otherwise it's almost dizzying. Readers know something's wrong, but they don't know what.

Frames, too, should be used properly. Like other elements, they should have a consistent style. Using different kinds of techniques can be distracting. Do something different only as an exception, to make a point.

On our cover, we use a four-color photograph with a white frame. That's different than many magazines, including trade publications, which tend to use a full bleed. Thus, the frame helps it to stand out among the competition. But it took a lot of trial and error on the part of our designer, production department, and printer to get it to trim right consistently.

One colleague says, if you can tell it visually, you should. Charts, tables, and graphs can quickly illustrate what might take paragraphs to explain. But the purpose must be clear: aiding communication.

Simple is better, but for charts, move beyond pies, fevers, and bars. Determine what's appropriate to the reader and the message. In keeping with your simple, consistent style, create a stylebook for graphics, especially if you do them often. Use the same fonts and sizes, weight of rules, color family, etc.

Putting It Together

When designs are done, look at them from the reader's point of view. The headline and hero shot have to jibe, otherwise it's sending a mixed message. The same goes for other display copy.

On the cover, especially, the words are as important as the image. Together they tell the story of the picture, why you should read this magazine. In *Chain Leader*, we try to show why this person deserves to be on the cover. We also use the stories' headlines as cover language, including page numbers, so readers can easily find what they're looking for.

In situations where text ends up either too short or too long, we first try to edit the text or adjust the layout, or both, depending on the story. When that isn't enough, we will be flexible with page counts, or perhaps add or subtract a partial-page ad.

Ways to further tighten already tight stories include using bulleted copy, because it packs more information into a small space. Plus, readers like it because it's scannable. In *Chain Leader,* we use a "Snapshot" box with at-a-glance information on each chain, which appears on almost all stories, even departments.

Don't duplicate information in display copy and text. This also adds to the value of the display copy. I know of a few magazines that don't ever allow information to be duplicated in body and display copy.

Reality check.   Since we all have the same access to the page layout, art directors can be tempted to adjust text, and editors can be tempted to adjust images to suit their own needs. Unless there is a clear understanding between the two, this must be avoided. For example, a deck or quote might look better if the lines were broken a certain way, but they might read better if whole phrases are kept on a single line. Re-cropping a photo, in order to add just a more few lines of copy, may mean having to rescale it and adjust rules, diminish balance on the page, or change emphasis in the image. Killing widows, those single words or the last syllable in a hyphenated word that are alone on the last line of a paragraph, can cause bad line breaks pages away. Even in a deadline rush, it's worth discussing it to avoid making a mistake.

Glossary of Terms

Here is a vocabulary list to aid in communication between editor and designer, which is key to successfully packaging a magazine.

Ascender: the part of a lowercase letter that goes above the base, as in b k l.

Base: the part of a lowercase letter that is the height of an x. Also called a letter's body, or x-height.

Bleed: to run a picture off the side of a page. Also used as a noun. A full bleed goes to the edge of all four sides of a page.

Body copy: the words of the main part of the story, as opposed to display copy.

Deck or deckhead: the copy that follows and expands on the headline, or that acts as display copy and selling point on subsequent pages of the story. Following the headline, it is sometimes called a subhead. On subsequent pages, it is sometimes called a blurb.

Descender: the part of a lowercase letter that goes below the base, as in j p y.

Display copy: decks, captions, quotes, etc., that draw in the reader, distinguished from body copy.

Em: the width of an uppercase M.

En: the width of an uppercase N.

Flush: aligned with. Flush left copy is aligned on the left and uneven on the right.

Font: a style of type, for example, Garamond Book Condensed. A font family has many styles, like all the different weights, widths, and versions of Helvetica.

Form: the large piece of paper on which several pages are printed, which is then folded and cut. Also called a signature.

Gutter: the margin of each page at the point of binding.

Hero shot: the most significant picture or piece of art telling the big part of the story.

Justify: align copy on both sides. Justified type has extra spaces inserted between words and letters to make that happen.

Leading: the space between the lines of copy. It is expressed as the size of type plus the space. 10/12, or 10 on 12, means 10-point type with two points of space between.

Perfect bound: stacks of pages are glued together at their edge, forming a spine.

Pica: a measurement equal to about one-sixth of an inch.

Point: a measurement. 12 points make up a pica; there are about 72 points in an inch.

Ragged: uneven lines. Ragged right, flush left means the left side of the text is justified, or aligned, and the right is not.

Reverse type: white copy on top of a photograph or other block of color.

Saddle stitch: binding of staples through the middle fold.

Serif: the cross line at the end of a stroke in a letter. Sans serif means without serif.

Side stitch: bound with staples through the stack of pages.

Sidebar: a related story set apart from the main story.

Signature: see Form.

Spread: two facing pages of a publication.

Subheads: small headings throughout body copy that provide entry points for the reader and break the story into more easily digestible sections. Also can be the display copy that follows and expands on the headline.

Widow: one word or the end of a hyphenated word left over at the end of a paragraph.

X-height: height of the lowercase x, which the type uses as its base.

Visual Design II

10

Making the Editor-Designer Marriage Work

Carol Holstead

It's tempting to think that because trade publications don't have to attract newsstand readers, their design isn't as important as their words. But they do still have to vie for attention on a reader's to-do list. If you want your magazine at the top of that list, you need to get involved in the design of your magazine. Here's how:

1. Learn to Think Like a Designer.

Marcus Villaca, creative director at Jungle Media Group, which publishes *Jungle* and *Jungle Law,* magazines for people new to business and legal professions, says there is a misconception between editors and art directors that one has some expertise that the other doesn't. "These days both editors and art directors have to learn the same sets of skills—editors have to think more visually and designers have to think about how to format copy that makes sense to the reader."

If you can, take a course in basic visual communication or publication design, which will teach you how to use type, art, and space effectively, and how to tailor your message to your audience. If you can't take a course, then read, said Rogier van Bakel, editor of *Jungle* magazine. Read design books and study all kinds of magazines, and ask yourself why a design succeeds or doesn't.

Villaca and van Bakel have backgrounds in design and journalism. Villaca has a bachelor's degree in journalism; van Bakel previously was editor of Advertising Age's *Creativity,* a magazine for art directors. Their experience makes it easier for them to collaborate and to develop appropriate treatments for stories, Villaca says. For example, when *Jungle Law* did a story on the inside of the Supreme Court, van Bakel's visual sense enabled him to see that an illustration would tell the story more effectively than copy. As a result, Villaca hired an illustrator to create a three-dimensional image of the court that formed the basis of the piece.

2. Collaborate in the Creative Process.

The best time to talk to a designer about how to illustrate a story is before it is written, says Lucia Carruthers, editor of *Winnipeg Women* and former projects editor for Veterinary Healthcare Communications. When she became editor of *Winnipeg*

Carol Holstead is associate professor of journalism at the University of Kansas.

Women, a magazine distributed free in Winnipeg, Canada, one of the first things she did was invite the art director to meetings with the head photographer to brainstorm story treatments.

"He had never been asked to do that before," she says. "We will talk about the story and what photographs are appropriate. The art director will often have different ideas from me, which is good. Many times we sketch out the page design before we take the pictures. We talk about every story and the artwork so there are no surprises when the art director gets all of the copy and art to design."

Like a lot of smaller magazines, *Winnipeg Women* is designed by a freelance art director, and he and Carruthers work out of separate offices. As a result, Carruthers has made a point of meeting with him face to face as often as possible, which allows them to communicate more easily than on the phone and by e-mail. She can also put a lot of design ideas in front of him. Carruthers keeps what she describes as a "massive file" of design examples culled from magazines to help her illustrate her ideas.

"When my art director sees what I like, and that I am invested in the design, it makes him want to impress me with his work, to wow me," she says.

3. Keep an Open Mind.

To collaborate fully, there needs to be a lot of give and take between you and your designer. Often when you begin working with an art director, you will have different visions of the magazine. It's important to try to set your own ideas aside and listen; and, of course, your art director has to listen to you.

Tammy Fernandez, art director of *American Demographics,* says she and her former managing editor, Suzanne Riss, were lucky—they had similar visions and respected each other from the start. Still they made an effort to listen to each other's ideas. Fernandez would listen to Riss's suggestions for art and Riss would listen to Fernandez's suggestions for story titles.

Everyone who reads a story will have a different take on it, and by exploring ideas with your designer, you will most likely arrive at the best treatment—the one most likely to reach your audience. Brainstorming together will also help foster an atmosphere of trust and respect so people feel free to express their ideas, Riss says.

Keeping an open mind means you also need to give your designer room to see an idea through, even if it doesn't appeal to you at first, because sometimes you have to see an idea on paper to believe in it, Riss says. Likewise, a designer should take the time to flesh out an editor's idea that may not appeal at first to see if it will work. "A good working relationship," says Riss, "is not about ego. It's about getting a good solution."

4. Show a Little Respect.

Recognize your art director's strengths and let her run with them, says Riss of *American Demographics.* Among Tammy Fernandez's strengths is working with illustration and photography, and knowing that helped Riss identify the design ideas that would most likely succeed. For example, when the two were having trouble figuring out how to illustrate a story about baby boomers hanging onto their youth, Fernandez came up with the idea to shoot a photo of a middle-aged man looking into a mirror and seeing a reflection of his younger self, a photo that in the wrong hands might have looked cheesy. "But I knew Tammy would make it elegant," Riss says.

Showing respect means not being territorial about the work, says van Bakel at *Jungle.* "Marcus (Villaca) is unbelievably good at writing headlines, and some editors would take offense at that," van Bakel says. When Villaca is roughing in a layout he will write a temporary title to go with the story, and van Bakel says the temporary headline often is better than anything he can come up with.

At *Winnipeg Women,* Carruthers tries to avoid telling her designer what to do. She says she will make suggestions—"I'll tell him what kind of design I had in mind when I wrote a headline"—but she won't dictate. If she believes a layout has problems, she will lead a discussion about it by asking her art director if he's happy with it. And when he does well, she makes sure to compliment him. "Lots of things have to be re-done, and positive reinforcement makes the revision less painful."

5. Hire Right.

Hiring a designer, if you have the chance, allows you to find someone who is a perfect fit for you and your publication. When considering applicants, you will not only conduct interviews, but will look at candidates' portfolios. Among the most important qualities to look for:

- Versatility in an applicant's work. Versatile approaches to design reveal that applicants have the tools to solve communications problems.
- A sense of humor, which is important not only in design but in working with a staff, van Bakel says.
- A visual sensibility similar to your own.
- An ego that is secondary to doing appropriate design. Designers who are just looking to advance their own careers are not thinking about what is best for the magazine, Villaca says.

For many editors and art directors, collaborating on a magazine's design is one of the best parts of their jobs because it's the point at which the editorial and visual elements coalesce. Both care passionately about what they do, but, as van Bakel says, they are willing to work as a team, which requires compromise and a recognition that collaboration can make the work better.

Feature Planning 11

A Cool, Deep, Nourishing Drink

Michael Lear-Olimpi

Editors wield a double-edged sword when they set out to develop a feature well for a trade publication. On the positive side, editors start with solid knowledge of what their readers want. Each trade publication has a ready-made topic in the field it covers. But here's the negative side: Knowing what your readers want can lead to a feature well that produces much of the same thing year after year. The challenge is to make industry-specific features sexy enough to appeal to the publication's audience while also making them accessible and—most critically—useful to readers, whether those readers are new to, or old hands at, their jobs.

How to Get Started

Building a deep well of must-read features provides you an opportunity to address your readers' basic needs, and it's essential to keep those needs in mind as you begin planning, whether for the year or for an individual issue.

For your readers, success in their profession, no matter what that profession is, depends on them delivering a high-quality product or service to someone—a customer, client, colleague, or superior. To that end, the feature well must be a storehouse of resources that can help readers do that, and to which they can return repeatedly for help. It's the evergreen nature of the feature well that largely sets it apart from other parts of a publication. News may be old a month after it's reported, and a column may be written to address a time-sensitive matter such as an upcoming conference or government action. But the usefulness of the core material covered in features lasts over time, even if some aspects of what's covered change.

So, editors must address up front in their planning one principal consideration: Which topics should features focus on over a certain time, typically a year?

Michael Lear-Olimpi, editor-in-chief of E-commerce Law & Strategy, *has taught journalism at Temple University. He is a former editor of national trade magazines and Web sites in logistics and healthcare, and has edited and reported for newspapers, including* The Philadelphia Inquirer.

Identifying Content

Long-term planning is the foundation for effective feature-well building, and the editorial calendar is the keystone to long-term planning. The calendar needn't be an unwieldy document that maps every detail for a year's worth of publication. Ideally, it should be a multi-slot picture frame with strong anchor articles that will attract readers, but be flexible enough for additions throughout the year as trends or industry changes emerge.

The well-stocked feature well also helps the editor maintain efficiency. Careful long-term planning that is the bedrock of crafting a calendar eliminates the need to plan each feature for every issue separately. This approach enables staff to meet production and delivery deadlines with fewer hurdles, and promotes content quality by reducing staff tension and burnout.

In devising a calendar, editors should count on one anchor feature, usually the cover story, and ideally at least two other features per issue. There's no formula for how many feature articles and which type should populate a trade publication, but, like in many aspects of life, variety is good. Some publishers apply a certain percentage of editorial-to-ad pages. In these cases, the number of features planned per issue depends on a publication's average folio, revenues, and staff.

The mix of article types? Personality profiles, investigative features, product-focused content, and other types of articles will hinge on which events occur and how important the editorial staff judges them to be, along with the editors' preferences for certain kinds of articles. Accessibility to sources or information might also be factors. Cover stories might be determined at the sessions, with a nod toward each second-place feature in the well and decisions on perhaps a how-to or technology piece.

One mix that has worked in a particular mid-sized publication (monthly, with an average of about 80 pages per issue) is a topic-specific cover story balanced by three or four supporting features. Each article should bring a unique perspective and be a different type of feature, such as a trend or how-to story.

In some publications, publishers require a mix, say a particular number of features covering product, people, and issues. If that's the case, then the planning focus might be limited to topics. But a staff's inventiveness can make even what appears a dry editorial mix interesting to readers by finding lively sources and new information, and applying active, engaging narrative technique and interesting, informative graphics.

Seven Tips for Building a Feature Well

1. Identify topics with special attraction to readers or advertisers.
2. Build in sidebars and related stories to highlight relevant products and services.
3. Tailor supplements and special sections to special interests and industry events.
4. Include sources from product companies in coverage.
5. Make a monthly summary of the upcoming issue for the sales staff to use.
6. Be open to the publisher's ideas and suggestions.
7. Be open to suggestions from sales representatives.

Some editors take the theme approach, at least for some issues, in which a theme is set and the features are linked with the cover story, which typically anchors the issue and sets the tone for the entire book.

An example is a publication for pharmaceutical company executives devoting an issue to drug development. The cover story gives an overview of recent drug developments, the second-place feature highlights ways drug companies finance clinical trials, and a third feature focuses on the role of technology in reducing the cost of drug trials. Other features in the issue don't touch on clinical trials, but highlight drug-development successes and leading researchers.

The process of identifying feature-story ideas is similar to the writing process:

Question: How does a B2B editor know when a feature idea should be turned into a feature story?
Answer: When he or she looks at it, perhaps for the second time, and says, "Wow, I didn't know that. That's terrific and I need to tell my readers."

An editor must trust her sense about what makes a story interesting. To tap into this subjective well of values, editors should engage in one of the few safe forms of assumption available to journalists: If an idea, looked at from a reader's perspective, is interesting, then readers probably will find the article built on the idea interesting.

Clearly, editors cannot stock their publications' calendars without knowing the industries they cover. Strong feature content reflects the events, personalities, and trends of the industry to which a particular magazine is devoted. For example, in many industries, markets go through seasonal peaks and valleys. For market sectors that depend on distribution—such as the retail industry—autumn is hiring season, when companies prepare for holiday shoppers' orders. In the building trades, companies might plan the start or completion of construction projects for the spring. And companies manufacturing outdoor recreation products such as bicycles and hiking gear target product launches by season, with cooler-weather products launching at the end of summer.

With their instincts as their starting point, editors should draw on every viable resource for feature-story ideas, beginning with the same basic story categories found in consumer publications, but with extra emphasis on how-tos, trends, and best practices. Some other categories: human-interest (dramatic events, interesting people); accomplishments; trendsetters; production facilities (if applicable to an audience); and products.

How-to articles are a staple in the trade-publication feature well, as are investigative stories shedding light on industry practices. Profiles of industry leaders are also common. During editorial-calendar development sessions, editors can eye the following sources for feature ideas:

The Market

Reporters often work beats, and editors should direct reporters to be vigilant in watching the market sectors they cover for feature ideas. With reporters acting as scouts, here's what typically emerges:

- *Trends.* What's different or being done in a different way?

- *Developments.* Inventions, new applications of products or theory, changes of industry job descriptions, or personnel titles or other nomenclature. Business, facility, or other property sales might fit this category. Maybe a sale or purchase was the largest of its kind, particularly difficult, involved a certain tax credit for the first time, or involved a unique workforce-sharing strategy.
- *News.* You wouldn't write a news story as a feature, but you might build a feature around a news story, in a sense "featurizing," or amplifying, some aspect of the news. One trade magazine for logistics managers ran a feature that touched on the Unabomber. It turns out a wood scientist at a center that developed pallets for warehousing and transportation tried to help the FBI track the bomber by analyzing wood fragments found at bombings. The scientist formed a guess on the specific part of the country in which the bomber might have lived and worked.
- *The unusual.* That same logistics publication constructed a feature out of where and how the rocks Apollo astronauts brought back to Earth are stored.

The Staff

Trade-publication editors and reporters should quickly become, if they don't start out that way, experts at identifying stories in the industries they cover. Some editorial directors or chief editors require staff, and occasionally freelancers, to suggest story ideas on a regular basis. Others tap staff and contributors for ideas monthly, weekly, or daily.

- *Idea rosters.* One way to accomplish this is for editors to ask each staff member, including the publisher, designers and, when feasible, salespeople for ideas for the annual or semiannual editorial-calendar planning meeting. Staffers should maintain a story log in which they jot down ideas whenever they occur. At some publications, chief editors or editorial directors require staff to submit rosters of monthly story ideas and a longer one prior to planning sessions. A database or similar file can be created in a publication's computer system or on an extranet that reporters and editors can access to contribute and examine feature-article ideas.
- *Notes.* Editors and reporters should keep lists of interesting aspects of stories they're developing for later treatment. These ideas can be fleshed out during regular story meetings or in specifically planned edition-building sessions.

Editorial Advisory Boards

Many publications maintain a stable of experts who are recognized leaders in the industries the publications cover to suggest story ideas, check articles for accuracy, be interviewed as story sources and help educate editors about the topics they cover.

These experts are a reservoir of feature-story ideas that should be tapped at least once a year, perhaps for input prior to an annual editorial-calendar planning session.

Some board members might want to write articles and should be encouraged to do so because their participation as writers provides publications with expert editorial and can lighten staff workload. If the board member is not a skilled journalist or writer, the publication's editors can assist in developing the piece, provide an outline, or ghost-write the article. Of course, the board member's contribution can be submitted in raw form, and the publication's staff can edit it into the proper style and direction.

Board members can also be invited to write supporting content, such as guest editorials, columns, and departments, to add depth to the feature. With columns and departments, topics can be planned well in advance to reflect edition themes or to reference feature topics to which editors want to call attention. (See Chapter 15 for an in-depth look at editorial advisory boards.)

Readers

A publication's editorial advisory board should consist of industry leaders, but rank-and-file subscribers—a publication's main audience—are also a source of story ideas. And many are happy to let editors know what they want to read, but editors have to ask them. Here are a few ways to do that:

- Put the e-mail address and phone number of an editor—preferably the chief editor—at the end of each article.
- With a print product, include the publication's Web site address on each page, and on that site offer readers a means of sending editors story ideas or for volunteering to write stories.
- Invite some readers to an editorial-calendar planning session. Some readers' companies or organizations will cover the expense of sending them to such a meeting, but for those who don't receive that benefit, the publication should foot the bill. Small publications can get around this possible cost problem by inviting local readers.
- Hold reader forums, with readers selected by editors or the publication's research staff, if it has one, at which participants discuss the kind of articles they expect the publication to offer.
- Establish a second editorial board, one of rank-and-file readers instead of industry leaders, to provide article-quality feedback and to suggest or produce stories.
- Include notices at the beginning or end of features inviting readers to submit article ideas or developed manuscripts.
- Hold a reader writing contest.

Conferences

Industry meetings are indispensable tributaries of ideas for the feature well of trade publications. They cannot be ignored. What kinds of stories do you get out of these meetings?

- *Advances.* These are previews of the conference, with programming and other high-interest information.
- *Follow-ups.* These are next-day or long-term features. Long-term features include articles produced throughout the year based on presentations, products, and interviews connected to the conference. Feature ideas could run the gamut from best practices to how-tos to profiles of conference presenters.
- *Product previews.* These look at products introduced at the exhibit hall or in sessions. A truly useful product could be a feature in itself, or several key time- and money-saving products could be the core of a product feature.
- *Product reviews.* These test and rate products introduced at the trade show.
- *Forums.* These are roundtables hosted by the editors to which industry leaders are invited. The idea is to gather exclusive editorial content. These forums can be presented live on the Internet or posted there later, and also turned into features or a series of features for later publication in the print magazine, online, or both.

Publication Archives

Editors should periodically review their publications' archives with an eye to revisiting past stories to update, extend or find new angles for them. This approach serves two basic purposes. It updates issues, and it helps publications confer "ownership" of issues by establishing certain types of stories as their exclusive domain.

A few examples of archive-based ideas include:

- *Industry growth.* Describing the demise of a part of or entire industry or market sector.
- *Retrospective.* A look back at industry milestones, including a "Who's where" of industry influencers and decision-makers.
- *Reexaminations.* Follow-up coverage of past news stories and reactions to events previously reported on, such as state officials' and local fire departments' response to the Three Mile Island nuclear accident in 1979 near Harrisburg, Pa.

Other Publications

Each editorial staff member should read the competition, and some noncompeting publications, to keep up with developments in the field he or she covers. It's unnecessary to say that editors shouldn't steal ideas from other publications, but they should watch for trends, people, and other feature ideas to which members of an editorial staff can apply their unique treatment.

Sometimes just reading good writing and reporting, or enjoying an attractive layout, will give editors an idea for their own publication.

Or perhaps a competitor's story will give editors an idea for something the story missed, or something related, in the competitor's piece.

The Advertising Connection

Don't neglect your publication's advertisers for story ideas. There's no reason not to tap your advertisers' expertise as long as the ground rules are clear to them about the inviolability of the editorial-advertising separation. Remember, your readers care about what your advertisers offer; if they didn't, advertisers wouldn't advertise, and the publication wouldn't survive. And advertisers are your readers, too.

In the end, a strong feature well is just that: a well. It's a place into which readers can dip again and again to satisfy their thirst for information and resources to help them do their jobs better. That's what trade publications are all about.

Like clean, cool water, the deep, well-stocked, nutritious feature well satisfies all.

See chapter exercise at the back of this book.

Government Coverage 12

Figuring Out Figureheads

John Latta

The government as covered by consumer media bears little resemblance to the government you read about in trade publications. The interest of the trade press, with its aim of providing practical information to its readers, is squarely focused on narrowly defined subjects, not subjects with broad social impact. The challenge for editors is to acquire knowledge of the workings of specialized areas of government and the organizations that work in those areas. There's little room for error.

Your readers are a tough, very educated, very interested audience compared to readers in the general press. Your readers factor the information you give them into their decision-making, and it's them—your readers—who commonly are the ones trying to shape policies of the lawmakers and government agencies you cover.

Because of their interest in the government matters on your beat, they have expectations about you. They consider you a fellow traveler on their road to success. In some manner, your readers expect you to approach your subject with the same concern that they do. If a government official says new rules will tighten certain procedures, your readers expect you to tell them not just the fact of the new rules but what they must do to comply with them, how the rules are expected to impact their industry, and what stakeholders are doing, if anything, to address them.

That said, in your quest to cover the news, it is essential to keep your reporting objective and let it be the industry, not you, that speaks through your pages.

The Beat of Government

Government is a beat, and you must be aware of all of the machinery of the beat. Nothing should happen on that beat that influences your industry that you're not aware of in advance.

There are times you will be surprised, but there shouldn't be many. There should be no individuals, committees, or agencies in decision-making positions that affect your industry that you aren't familiar with. Arriving at this level of awareness requires you to dig for information even when you're not pursuing a particular story, because covering government affairs for a narrow, educated, interested audience means being

---

John Latta is executive editor of Truckers News, *Randall Publishing, Tuscaloosa, Ala., and adjunct instructor of journalism, University of Alabama.*

aware that almost any move by the people you cover could affect some of your readers in some way at some time.

That said, learning your beat requires learning about the people in your industry, their organizations, and the lawmakers and officials that impact them:

- Who are the lobbyists and public advocates in your field, what are their priorities, and how do they engage with lawmakers and government officials?
- How does the economy, in macro and micro terms, interact with your industry? For example, what are the indicators in your industry that the government relies on to gauge how the economy is functioning? What impacts the data of those indicators?
- What is the regulatory perspective of the agencies you cover? Have they traditionally leaned toward or away from regulation?

Seeking mastery of this information is crucial if you're to have the skills to follow a paper trail. How else will you know that something is out of place and needs looking into? How else will you know that a provision hidden away on page 16 of a regulatory board's report has the power to change your industry?

Beat Organization

To get started, create a chart to keep track of the operations of key committees, boards, agencies, and associations until you're familiar enough with them that you can track them unaided. A flow chart can help you see where things are and appear to be going. It can alert you that a step in a government process has been missed—a tip-off to something out of the ordinary happening. The chart should include every moving piece of the industry you're covering, including the activity of lobby groups and business associations.

Keep a calendar, too. It saves you from a most basic mistake—missing a meeting, report publication date, or a deadline.

Sources

Whether you latch onto a story yourself or a story is handed to you, you'll need to obtain official and unofficial commentary to piece together the full picture behind the story. The official commentary tells you how an agency or interest group wants to position itself on an issue, while the unofficial commentary gives you the context of what is happening. This is especially important in a trade publication context, because the official position is typically aimed at a general audience, which is not your audience. At the same time, to report on the unofficial commentary without acknowledging the public stance can leave your coverage deficient in a crucial way.

For that reason, it's best to follow up news generated by principal government officials or industry leaders by talking to the people behind the scenes. Don't accept the remarks of the one without referring to the insight of the other.

"The actions of lawmakers and regulators are typically aimed at a consumer audience, so whether it's a bill in Congress or a notice of proposed rulemaking from a federal agency, the news at the industry level is usually buried in the press materials—or perhaps omitted altogether," says Avery Vise, editorial director of *Commercial Carrier Journal,* which covers the trucking industry for executives and managers. "To ensure that business journalists catch every industry concern, they need to follow up with staff for the appropriate officials and scan the legislation or proposed rules themselves." Vise is a long-time trade publication editor with roots in covering the government for industries.

At the same time, don't rely on the obvious sources for your commentary and background information. Identify those players who are less central to your beat but who might be of help to you. There may be more of these in government circles than in other beats, because many different interests will have different stakes in an issue, and these different interests will have different motivations for circulating information around an industry.

Effective editors will tell you that they maintain sources—an agency bureaucrat, industry attorney, secretary, mid-level assistant—that no one would ever think of as being sources but who are key to getting to the bottom of events. "The behind-the-scenes people are the people who really know what your readers need to know," says Vise.

What's more, these sources are likely to have a strong sense of why it's important to get their message out to a trade publication. High-level officials, with their focus on a broad constituency, may not see the benefit to talking to a trade publication editor. That may be short-sighted on their part, but it's the environment in which you work. So, other sources are key. "There's an inverse relationship between the stature of the official you would like to quote and the willingness of that person to make time for an industry-specific publication," says Vise. "Without the profile that comes with affiliation with a major news outlet, business publication journalists don't always find officials accessible."

Although it's important to cultivate these strong background sources, always be looking for new ones. You need new points of view to keep your understanding of issues fresh. New sources, particularly those coming at issues from a different vantage point, can alert you to developments that you wouldn't be expected to recognize through your regular contacts. A subcommittee looking at baby formula labeling, for example, may throw something into a bill on school lunch programs that changes the way teachers are paid. Sources from outside your industry can keep you informed on these developments that take place on the sidelines.

To keep track of everyone you know, create a database of your sources and your potential sources and plug them in.

What to Report

If you cover your beat effectively, you become in some measure an expert, someone who knows more about a subject than many in your readership. This is true with any beat but especially so with government coverage, since matters of law and regulation that affect an industry are rarely the central focus of your readers, whose attention is appropriately on the core of their business. Thus, they look to you to support your coverage with interpretation, background, and projection—value-added information that they can act on.

That said, how much background and interpretation you provide is a challenge. Your readers have distinct needs and approach your material from different positions and levels of experience. "One of the greatest challenges in covering government for an industry publication is knowing when you are providing too little detail and when you are providing too much," says Vise.

Stories need depth so that the CEO of one company and the administrator of another, or an investor in one company and a middle level manager of a trade association, can see how an issue affects them. But what that depth is will be different for each of them.

What to do? Take some time to look at your publication's audits or any other research into your readership. It's not enough to say that all your readers are executives in a given industry. You will commonly face a problem of writing a story where a good part of your audience will be well versed in a subject, but another good-sized part of it may not be. You have to consider including explanations or background paragraphs that may be assumed by some readers but that, if left out, would leave others bewildered.

"Taxes, appropriations, authorization bills, rules, and so on can be as simple or as complex as you want to make them," says Vise. "You need to know the readers' degree of sophistication and their level of interest in the details. If your readers are primarily big-picture people—chief executives, corporate vice presidents—an emphasis on the legislative or regulatory process likely will not help them. They need information they can act on. At the other extreme are lobbyists and advocates, who need to keep close watch on the process. Many of them already know what you will write—or at least think they do."

In practice, your frequency of publication may be an important consideration in deciding how much attention to devote to process. A daily or weekly publication focuses more on process than a monthly, because in daily and weekly increments it's often the process that constitutes the news. If you're a monthly with daily news online, editors need to pay attention to both policy and process. If you're just a monthly, focus on outcomes, not process.

Present It with Spirit

There is a tendency by some editors to consider government coverage important but stiff. Work hard to make your coverage interesting. To be sure, the lawmakers, public officials, and staff you deal with won't necessarily have the profile of presidential candidates, but trade editors aren't necessarily serving their readers if they don't allow personality and color to enter into their coverage. It's okay to take a cue from the consumer press here.

In its coverage of the 2002 Florida gubernatorial election, *Florida Trend* magazine used colorful cover language—"Five imminent crises that will create big headaches for Florida's next governor"—and an action-oriented angle to create a high-value package of information for its readers, who are Florida business executives.

Another story, "Battening Down The Hatches," compared one year's budget crisis to the one from the previous year and began the story with an easy-to-grasp mathematical formula.

The writing and presentation adopted ideas from the consumer press to good effect and without diminishing the seriousness and usefulness of the information, indeed making it more compelling and thereby making it more likely to be more widely read.

A few other thoughts on presentation:

- *Avoid jargon.* Government is awash with jargon, and too much of it appears in print. Editors should assume their readers aren't familiar with the terms and avoid using them.
- *Avoid acronyms.* Reliance on acronyms can cloud the readability of your coverage.
- *Think art.* Think in terms of breaking down coverage in a main bar, sidebars, boxes, and visuals such as a checklist of key legislative provisions, comparisons of bills, or bullet points on how a proposal would impact an industry.

Help Your Readers

Much of what you cover is complex and needs explanation, and you're trying to help your readers understand how government actions affect them, what they must do to stay in compliance, and where they can look in seeking changes to the law. Measured by this task, you are an industry's educator on government matters. Assume readers, having gone into your industry without background in the relevant government issues, will look to your publication to become more educated about the matters. They're a tough, very educated, very interested audience, and that gives you an opportunity to provide coverage that makes a difference to them.

Concluding Information

The Missing Link: Quantitative Analysis

Covering government means covering numbers. Lawmakers and agencies build public policies around numbers. The programs they devise are designed to meet certain needs, and in identifying those needs, they rely on research and make certain assumptions. How many people are without health insurance? What is the scope of the problem? Exactly how large is a $2.1 billion budget deficit? How many school lunches can a $1 million program budget buy?

How "numerate" are trade publication editors? Not very—but the same can be said for reporters and editors in all areas of journalism.

"Journalists of all kinds today, not just business publication journalists, need training in quantitative analysis," says Ed Mullins, chairman of the Department of Journalism and Behringer Professor of Communication at the University of Alabama. "Very few journalists today know how to find and analyze data necessary to assess business conditions astutely.

"My biggest concern with journalists is their failure to use available quantitative evidence to support or reject the stated and unstated hypotheses we include in our stories all the time. We don't disclose our methods, and when we do we don't show the numeric basis of them often enough, because though highly literate, most journalists are innumerate. Actually, as I think of my coinage, I don't think you can be literate without also being numerate. Proof of the de-emphasis of number thinking in humanity is the familiarity with a concept about literacy but not even a familiar word for its numeric equivalent."

There are a number of basic computer applications (Excel, Access) that give one a start to organizing and interpreting data and others (SPSS and SASS) that enable the user to assess relationships. They are programs that people of ordinary literacy can learn to use. "Business schools," says Mullins, "teach the use of these tools but few journalism schools do. So business sources are usually ahead of journalists. And that's not a good thing."

10 Web Sites for Covering the Federal Government

Note: The precise URL for these websites may change over time as the host organizations adopt new Web technology. These addresses are current as of November 2003. List compiled by Avery Vise, editorial director of *Commercial Carrier Journal.*

1. GPO Access *(www.gpoaccess.gov)*—A service of the Government Printing Office, I consider this the government reporting super site. It features links to keyword search engines for all the official federal legislative and executive publications, such as the *Federal Register* and *Congressional Record,* and it offers links to government documents by topic.

2. Thomas *(thomas.loc.gov)*—A service of the Library of Congress, Thomas provides a more robust collection of search options than GPO Access for documents related to Congressional proceedings.

3. Office of the Federal Register *(www.archives.gov/federal_register)*—The most useful feature of this site, which is maintained by the National Archives & Records Administration, is the public inspection list—a rundown of documents filed for publication in the *Federal Register* and available for public viewing at the Office of the Federal Register. Routine or relatively minor documents are placed on public display the day before publication. More significant rulemakings may be available for public view as much as a week in advance. Another useful resource is a link to a searchable Electronic Code of Federal Regulations that is current to within a couple of days.

4. Office of Management and Budget Regulatory Matters page *(www.whitehouse.gov/omb/inforeg/regpol.html)*—Useful mostly as a medium- to long-range planning tool, OMB's website provides the status of federal regulations that have been drafted by federal agencies but not yet formally proposed. The most valuable resources are the pages showing regulations that have been submitted for White House review and those that have been cleared within 30 days. This service gives the journalist a few weeks or even months to gather background material on a proposed or final rule.

5. FirstGov.gov *(www.firstgov.gov)*—Billed as "the U.S. Government's Official Web Portal," *firstgov.gov* is probably the most comprehensive website for finding information in all branches of government. If all else fails, you should be able to click your way through to the information you need—eventually.

6. The White House *(www.whitehouse.gov)*—Don't have White House credentials? The official Web site is practically as good as being there, especially if you aren't on a daily or hourly news cycle. The Web site provides news releases, nominations, executive orders and so on. You can even read transcripts of daily press briefings.

7. The news wires *(www.prnewswire.com, www.businesswire.com, www.usnewswire.com)*—If a player in your industry issues a press release on a government matter, you probably will find it at one of these sites. Access is free for most services, and working journalists can sign up for additional free resources and capabilities on some of the sites.

8. National Contact Center *(www.pueblo.gsa.gov/call/pressreleases.htm)*—A service of GSA's Federal Citizen Information Center in Pueblo, Colo., this Web site maintains a list of news release websites for all the government agencies.

9. General Accounting Office *(www.gao.gov)*—When things are slow elsewhere in government, it's always nice to fall back on a juicy report from Congress's federal agency watchdog. The Web site allows you to sign up for e-mail notification of reports issued by industry.

10. The Library of Congress *(www.loc.gov)*—It's often useful to provide readers an historical context, and there's no better resource than Congress's own library.

Web Publications   13

New Thinking for a Broad Canvas

"People don't read online."

"If you're creating content for the Web, keep it short and simple."

*"A print publication is more serious and sophisticated
than an online publication, and the standards
for a print publication must be higher."*

"If it doesn't fit in print, put it online."

—Todd Raphael

As a Web editor, I've been hearing all of the above in one form or another for years. There isn't much truth to any of them. The principles of great journalism—useful content, compelling stories, separation of advertising and editorial, accuracy—are every bit as true online as they are in print. That's as much the case for online trade journalism as for consumer journalism.

That said, Web and print publications are very different from each other, and it's in this difference that editors of trade publications can generate value for their readers far beyond what they could do solely though a print publication.

As a trade publication editor, you're goal is to help your readers thrive in their profession, whatever that profession is. That goal is what effectively separates trade from consumer journalism, and it's also what makes the online medium a natural extension of the value-added content that trade publications aim to provide. Indeed, a Web publication is ideally suited as a resource for the practical, useful, and interactive content for readers that print publications aren't well structured to provide.

What You Can Do Online

When you enter the online world, you begin to think of editorial issues in a different way than you're used to in print.

Margaret Magnus, who for many years was the publisher and CEO of *Workforce.com,* an online trade publication on the human resources industry, believes that "editorial" is an incomplete way of describing the information posted at your online publication.

Her preferred word is "content." Content encompasses more than just written narrative. It includes bulletin-board postings or user chat sessions. It may include audio or

---

Todd Raphael is online editor at Workforce Management, *a Crain Communications publication.*

video. Editorial conjures up an image of an article; online, you may have content that includes no words but is merely a calculator. Content is a better way of describing what you can do online, and it opens up opportunities for presenting useful information to readers who are hungry for material that can give them an edge in their industry or profession.

The parameters of print are clear. A magazine editor can provide a reader with 300 words or 1,000 words or 2,500 words on a given subject. The editor must choose what's most important to readers at a given time.

An online editor faces a different task—providing content that, over time, provides much of what a reader needs to know about a subject. That's a far taller order, but it's not necessarily a more daunting one. The online editor has a broader canvas on which to work.

Try this exercise: pick a subject, any subject. Imagine what a reader would want to know about it. Over time, you can assign this content. Let's try it with the subject of coaching track and field. Assume your readers are track coaches or aspiring track coaches. Here is some of the content you might offer readers:

- profiles of interesting coaches
- information on getting certified and learning CPR and other first aid basics
- comparisons of coaching high school vs. junior high vs. college track
- comparisons of coaching track at a major school (such as a Division I college) vs. a small school (and a similar comparison for high schools)
- updated techniques for coaching such as how to use the latest starting blocks for sprinters
- lists of coaches, with links to their teams' Web sites (for job hunters)
- information about conventions and trade shows for the industry
- product and service vendor information—track shoes, for example, or stop watches
- techniques for coaching shot put, high jump, long jump, discus, hammer throw, pole vault, and javelin

Showcase value-added content. Web-based trade publications are ideally suited to provide the practical and useful content that print publications can't effectively provide because of space limitations and the absence of real-time interactivity.

Screenshots from *www.workforce.com*. Used with permission.

- bulletin boards and Webinars (online seminar) for coaches to discuss common challenges
- articles on highly regarded coaches around the world
- sample spreadsheets for designing track practices (plug in your desired time for a given event to generate a practice for each day of the week)
- list of coaching job openings
- audio and video interviews with coaches
- video providing instruction on coaching methods
- tips on breaking into the field of coaching, advice about what skills are needed, and what you can expect from a coaching job
- printable worksheets a coach or athlete could use to keep track of athletes' times and progress throughout the season.

This is an exercise to use for whatever industry you're in. You can take a sliver of your industry and consider everything your audience wants and needs to know. Over time, assign this content piece by piece, solidifying your site as a valuable destination on the Web for your industry.

What's key here is the extent to which the range and depth of content goes beyond what can be effectively presented in print. Certainly you can provide sample spreadsheets in a print magazine, but do you want to devote so much of a finite resource to that kind of material? What about job listings, which can be updated daily online? Can a print publication effectively compete with that, and, if so, should it use its resources in that way?

But to tap online capabilities fully, editors need to shed print-based planning ideas and think in broader terms. As a starting point, consider questions that help you get at the differences between print and Web publications. You may not have all the answers, but if these questions represent the sort of exploration you're doing as a manager or editor of a Web site, you're doing something right.

Questions to Ask

Where are the users? These are the people you want to drive to your site. What print magazines do they read? What Web sites do they use? How will you bring them to your site?

What do your users want? What do they need? What products and services do they buy? What can you do to make their jobs easier?

What's the goal of your Web site? Is it a supplement to a print publication? Is it an alternative to a print publication? How will your users use each? Will they use them together as a combined tool?

Is interactivity in your sights? How will you best take advantage of the interactivity of the Internet to the benefit of your users? How will you use its many dimensions, from audio to video, from Webinars (Web-based seminars) to traditional articles?

How will you handle user feedback? How will you use it to strengthen the relationship between you and them?

Who are your key industry vendors? Are you getting good information from them about trends in your field, about important decision-makers you should be in touch with?

Is your site providing more than text and narrative? What tools are you offering? Do you still think of your publication as a magazine and not as a tool? Are you providing just an online magazine or is it something more?

What's your content shelf life? Is the information you're putting online going to be relevant when a search is conducted a month later? A year later? How long do you want your content to be online? Will it still be current at that point?

Does your audience read online? How much do they read online, and how much will they read online? How many words are too many? How many are too few? Are you "dumbing down" your content to put it online, or putting the "leftovers" online? Are you holding the Internet to the same standards as you do ink and paper?

What is your relationship with the print staff? Do you cooperate or compete with the staff from your related print publication? Or, if your staff is not separated (print people and online people), should it be? Does your staff configuration mirror the goals of your company as a multimedia product?

Building Traffic and Creating a Community

Once you consider basic questions such as these, you can flesh out your site content, starting with the help of the users who form your online community.

One of the distinctive characters of the online environment is the sense of community of people who spend time at a site. Print publications attract readers, but Web publications cultivate a community, and in trade publications, that community is held together by a shared interest in an industry or profession. A Web publication with a strong community generates high traffic volume. How do you manage your content to build traffic? You can start by tapping key members of the community you want to reach.

Political campaign managers will tell you that one endorsement from a member of the school board, the Kiwanis, or the Rotary is worth dozens of endorsements from a less-active citizen. That's because active community members hold enormous influence over hundreds of other voters.

A Web site works the same way. To build content, focus on the most critical customers.

Round Up the Surfers

Spend some time in Google's bulletin-board search function (if you have an intern, this is a great job for them) finding some of the people who are active posters on var-

Community centric. Identify the people in your industry who are active online and make them your first line of feedback as you structure your Web publication. Then, keep them active with a robust online community center. Online interaction is one of the principal ways publications on the Web distinguish themselves from publications in print, so make your online community a centerpiece for your industry.

Screenshots from *www.workforce.com*. Used with permission.

ious bulletin boards that cover your industry. These are the people you want on your site. These are the places you want to advertise to bring people to your site.

Milk Feedback for All It's Worth

Two types of people will e-mail you with a question. The first are hard-core site users. The second kind could become so. Take time to research their questions, and you'll create a user who knows where to get help. Since that user wasn't shy about asking you for help, they probably won't be shy about telling others where the info came from. Also, ask them for input on the site—it's a free focus group.

Use Vendors

Next time you're chatting with one of the vendors in the field covered by your publication, ask if they've received any good leads from users who clicked through from your site to theirs. Then—assuming the vendor calls that customer ahead of time and is okay with you calling them—contact that lead, asking how their experience was with your site. A user thinking of making a purchase is a user who will make another purchase. You want these people coming back.

Reward People

When each of your users hits their anniversary (each year they've been registered with you), send them an e-mail thanking them, and ask them what more you can do to serve them. If you charge for the site, send them a certificate or coupon. Also, reward frequent site users for their business. I once sent a very frequent site user an Amazon gift certificate to thank him for his business. He used it to buy a book about management, and shared what he learned with the rest of the *Workforce.com* community.

Hold Focus Groups, in Person or Online

Before you make changes to your site, bring together a few users for an online chat, an audio conference call, or an in-person focus group. Ask them how the site could be better. Ask how the navigation could be better. More importantly, ask how they use the site, what they want from the site, and what will help them do their jobs better. Ask what you can do to make them look good!

Watch the Traffic Reports

I regularly monitor the traffic reports of our site, reports that show the most popular items among our users. Try to offer more of what people want and less of what they don't. Be careful: appealing to a large number of people shouldn't always be your goal. Honda was successful selling the Accord to many, but Jaguar was also successful selling the XKE to the few. You may want to offer some "premium value" (possibly paid) content that appeals to a narrower section of people and some content that appeals to a larger group.

News Content

Many Web sites post news daily, and some even several times a day. Others have set up automatic systems for e-mailing news to self-selected subscribers each time a story is posted on the site.

If you do this, you'll have the choice of having your staff write their own frequent news stories to post, or using one of several syndicated services. If at all possible, write your own.

Mass-produced stories can be dry. They're also not tailored specifically to your readership. What's more, they can't be expected to provide the same connection with your readers as stories your staff write.

But be accurate. The more often that you write, the quicker you write, the greater potential for error. Balance the need for quality with the need for speed when you're producing content for online. More isn't always better.

Access Charges

It's an unsettled question among those in Web publishing: should something be free, just because it's online? Why should print content be paid content and online content be free?

The reality is, people expect at least some online content to be free, and they're not going to part with their money for information that isn't valuable to them professionally. At the same time, information has value, and publishers want to tap that value.

One way to test the money waters is by offering some of your information for free. At other parts of your site, you can charge a monthly fee, an annual fee, or a per-article fee, or require that users be subscribed to your print publication.

As editor, you should be working closely with others in your company such as your chief financial officer or head of marketing to make a strategy on paid content work. It may be a strategy that relies 100 percent on paid content (with no advertising), 100 percent on advertising (with no paid content), or some combination thereof. It may rely on the sale of products on your site.

The important thing is that you have a seat at the table when this strategy is developed and implemented. You'll need to advocate for the same things a print editor would advocate for—separation of advertising and editorial, high quality content, and a clear mission for your site that users understand.

E-mail Newsletters

The best way to remind your audience that your site is useful to them is by e-mailing them regularly with compelling information. E-mail newsletters are wonderful because you can measure the click-through rate of links, and in an instant see which pieces of content that you push to users are of most interest to them.

Here are some items you may want to include in an e-mail newsletter to your users:

- links to new articles on your site
- links to new products available on your site
- links to other sites. Let's say your Web site covers the fashion industry. If there's a great article in *Entertainment Weekly* about fashion, you may want to insert a link to it in your e-mail newsletter. You didn't write the article, but you can provide a useful service to readers by saying to them, "I've scoured the Web, and here are the best articles I found."
- short interviews, anecdotes, humor, and quotes
- tips on getting the most out of your site, navigating the site, or lists of most popular items and most frequent questions
- links to bulletin-board posts that are drawing interesting discussions
- profiles of new members, interesting members, or well-known users of your site
- information on events, seminars, training opportunities, and other high-interest goings-on.

If you want ideas on what to put in your e-mail newsletter, look at other newsletters and consider which ideas would work for your site.

At *Workforce.com,* we publish three e-mail newsletters, with more slated to come. Workforce Week features a combination of links to new site items, hot bulletin board posts, interviews I conduct with leaders in business, and news, both serious and light. "Dear Workforce" is in a "Dear Abby" format that turns reader questions into answers that are of interest to other readers. "Workforce Recruiting" is our first newsletter aimed at a segment of our market, people who are trying to make their companies known as great places to work.

Commerce

Organization in print is pretty simple—you have ads in one place, and in another, you have editorial. Online, it's a different story.

It's easier for people to purchase a product or service when they see something they want online than when they're flipping through a magazine, because the mechanism for ordering is right there. They don't have to put the magazine down and go

Vendor listings add dynamism. On the Web as in print, the separation of editorial from advertising content is an inviolable principle. At the same time, advertisers can provide content that is highly sought after by your readers. After all, learning about new industry products and services is a main reason why readers turn to trade publications. Help your readers access your advertisers with vendor listings. Just make sure you clearly identify them for what they are.

Screenshots from *www.workforce.com.* Used with permission.

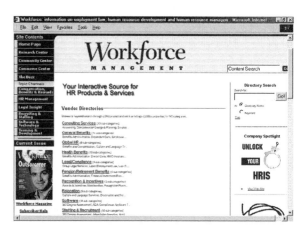

somewhere to do something. With that in mind, there's a role for editors in helping them make that decision to purchase—or not.

Workforce.com ran a feature about assessment tools. These are the tests-personality tests, skills tests, honesty test, and more—that employers use to help winnow down a list of candidates to a final few they want to interview. Along with the feature, we offered users a link to a section of our Commerce Center—an online product directory that contained a listing of vendors hawking tests and other assessment tools.

You'll want to think about the words you use to clearly indicate to readers that they're searching through a directory of products in which people have paid to be included. You can say it's a "vendor listing," a "paid listing," an "advertiser section," and so on.

If you're going to do product reviews, you'll want to clearly state for your readers that these reviews are done by the editorial staff (if they are) and aren't advertising. You'll want to be careful that your reviews aren't influenced by who is and isn't an advertiser, or how big of an advertiser they are.

Concluding Notes

Do You Need to Be a Techie?

If you're new to the Web content world, you may be wondering: How much do I need to know about technology? Do I need to know how to build Web sites?

It depends. It depends on the company you work for, the job you want to get, the path you want to take, and more. As a general rule, think of it this way: for print editors to move up the ranks, they should supplement their editing background with a basic understanding of design, circulation, and print production. That said, print editors don't need to memorize postal rates or be highly skilled at, say, Photoshop, a key part of standard publishing software. But they do need to know enough about those aspects of publishing to factor them into their thinking.

The same goes for you. You should have, at a minimum, an idea of how a Web site is built, how much technologies that could be added to site cost, and how the site's search mechanism operates. Stay updated on the latest technology available. But don't worry about learning to be a programmer.

You must be involved in all site design changes. Don't let your information technology department hijack the process.

What's This "Content Management System" Thing?

If you haven't heard of a "content management system" yet, you probably will soon.

This is the principal technology for adding articles and other material to your Web site. You use it to schedule when material goes on and off the site, designate where on the site the material should go, and add photos, hyperlinks, and sidebars to online articles.

As a Web editor, you should be involved in the selection of your company's content management system, as well as in the process of upgrading the system. You'll want to be sure your technology department knows what you'd like the system to do.

Bulletin Boards: A Voice of Moderation

Many Web editors moderate bulletin board on their Web sites. They ask thought-provoking questions. Or, they advise users on how to find answers to their questions on the site.

If you moderate a bulletin board on your Web site, talk to your company's attorney first. The laws regarding online content are fluid, but expect that the more you take a "moderating" role in managing a bulletin board, the more responsibility you bear.

continued

If someone posts something libelous or slanderous, it's easier to say in a court of law that "this is my readers' bulletin board, I don't run it and control what goes on there," if such a statement is actually true. Consider structuring your bulletin board so you can say that.

To See or Not to See

Think of your Web site as an environment with three dimensions—audio, video, and written text. When you're designing a feature article, consider all three dimensions.

Let's say your Web site covers the stock market. Some ideas for using audio and video:

- Interview stock pickers and provide the audio online.
- Show footage that tells a story supplementing your articles. If the article is on customer service problems at a grocery-store chain, provide film of customer service at the store.
- Provide the audio of conference calls held by corporations.
- Offer audio or video of important corporate events relevant to your articles. If a CEO of a software company gave an important speech to employees regarding the company's new products, put the audio and video on your site.
- Hold an online Webinar to educate your readers on a topic, enabling them to ask questions by phone or by e-mail during the session.

Freelancers

14

Hiring and Managing for Success: Six Tips
Alan R. Earls

Freelancers are crucial to the trade press. Little industry-wide data exist, but many trade publication editors tap the work of paid freelancers at least occasionally, and some rely on them extensively.

What's clear is that, with budgets tight at many publications, freelancers are a key resource for editors in handling peak workloads, reporting on special topics, or serving as a flexible element in a publication's staffing strategy. In addition to saving publishers money on benefits, insurance, and office space, freelancers are likely to be highly motivated. They're independent businesspeople that earn their income by satisfying you, the editor, so they come wanting to make a mark. With encouragement, freelancers can function as adjunct staff—crafting great articles, smoking out stories, and generating fresh ideas.

Finding Writers

However, the specialized work demanded by business, trade, and association publications means good freelancers aren't easy to find. You can locate freelancers by advertising in journalism publications, contacting freelancer associations, and monitoring other publications for writers whose work appears to have the qualities you need. In a crunch, you may need to cultivate writers with little experience in the industry you cover. If these writers are guided sufficiently, that shouldn't be a problem. If a writer comes to you with the right skills, they can do the job. Whether they're ferreting out facts about a town's mayor or exploring the industry-wide implications of a product change, the skills are the same.

Setting the Stage

In getting started, ask writers for article clips. You can also ask for professional references, though editors generally find this information less informative for their purposes than the clips. Start them on less challenging assignments while encouraging them to become familiar with your audience and industry.

Alan R. Earls, a former trade publication editor and publisher, is a freelance editor and writer based in Franklin, Mass. His clients include publications in the trade and consumer press.

Structuring Fees

Compensation for freelancers varies widely. It's not uncommon for publications to pay anywhere from 50 cents to $1 a word, or from a few hundred dollars to $1,000 or more per article. Try to find out what competing publications pay and pay similar rates, if you can. You may have to offer more to attract the most skilled writers.

Maintaining Quality

Managing freelancers for the business and trade press is straightforward. Unlike employees, with their varied responsibilities, some of which may be hard to measure or assess, freelancers are managed and evaluated on the basis of one story at a time. They will focus single-mindedly on that task. It is up to the editor to evaluate the effort effectively.

Given their fee-based compensation, freelancers are highly sensitive to time use. Set reasonable expectations and be as clear as possible about what's required. To ensure that your freelancer delivers what you want, be sure to provide, at a minimum, an assignment letter describing the article, expected word count, ownership of rights, deadlines, and compensation). In addition, provide a detailed story description or outline, sometimes including a source list and a discussion of the crucial points that must be gleaned from the sources. When done thoroughly, the assignment can help ensure that a first draft comes close to being the finished product you want. But that's not the end of the process. It is also important to be clear on your editing and revision cycle so that freelancers can plan their time.

Handling Revisions

Again, recognize that the freelancer is being paid on a fee basis. Freelancers expect to provide corrections and revisions—if what's requested is reasonable. Work to avoid the frustrations that come with multiple revisions, and you'll be on your way to forging a productive, long-term relationship with a freelancer. In all cases, be sure you understand the specific differences that must be recognized between freelancers and employees in terms of acceptable degrees of supervision, location of work, and the degree of independence exercised.

Avoiding Snags

Although not commonly a problem, some editors worry about conflicts of interest. For instance, do the freelancers have a relationship with an organization they're asked to write about? Have they signed non-disclosure agreements with companies that would prevent them from delivering effective reporting? Or will they take the information generated for you and retail it to a competing publication? While these issues rarely present a problem, they're concerns that you need to address in the terms of an assignment letter.

Editorial Advisory Boards

15

At the Crossroads of Information and Expertise

Robin Sherman

For many trade publications, the place where journalism and industry expertise meet is the editorial advisory board. Editors look to the boards for help in shaping the content and enhancing the credibility of their publication. Board members gain an opportunity to provide advice on the exchange of information in their industry.

Not all publications maintain an editorial advisory board, of course, and for those that do, how the boards are structured, who sits on them, and how much influence they wield differ widely.

What's clear, though, is that, for those that use them, editorial advisory boards can be effective sources for well-targeted content as long as the duties of the board are strictly defined and its members selected to represent a broad cross-section of an industry. When these two characteristics aren't met, boards at best lack relevance and at worse hobble an editor.

Those are some conclusions drawn from a survey on editorial advisory boards conducted in 2003 by the American Society of Business Publication Editors.

Here's how editors of trade publications are using boards, and, of those who don't use them, why they don't. Survey results are based on responses from 164 editors from a survey sample of 432 trade publication editors with membership in ASBPE, for a 38 percent response rate.

Tapping Industry Expertise

Most trade publication editors work with an editorial advisory board in some capacity if the ASBPE results are taken as representative of trade publications as a whole. ASBPE members are editors of trade, business, and association magazines and their associated Internet publications, and are based throughout the United States.

In the survey, about two-thirds of editors work with a board, mainly to capture ideas for articles and to chart publication direction.

Robin Sherman is ASBPE associate director and principal, Editorial and Design Services, Atlanta, Ga. Sherman is a former corporate editorial director at Argus, Inc. (now part of Primedia Inc.), publisher of more than 50 trade publications.

For these editors, the expert board helps them compensate for the lack of industry expertise they bring to their magazine coverage. "We are a trade medical publication," one editor in the survey says. "Many of us don't have formal medical or scientific training, so our editorial board helps to ensure our articles are factually and scientifically accurate."

The boards also help editors plug a hole in expertise when they lose an experienced person. "We used to have an engineering editor," one editor says. "He retired. We couldn't hire someone quickly and lost the position entirely. The board helps fill that role."

Even where they're considered industry experts in their own right, either through background or years of writing about an industry, editors don't work in the field every day, and therefore rely on others for up-to-date information. "Having a group to bounce ideas off of is great," one editor says.

That outside expertise may also validate the publication's authority. "The respected names in our publication are an objective eye that keep us on our toes," says an editor. "That gives us independent credibility."

Editors find that maintaining a board can provide them with benefits in any number of ways:

Unfamiliar coverage areas: The board can act as a sounding board for article ideas before editors move into an area new to them.

Political cover: Editors can arm themselves with some protection against industry fallout when the board signs off on a controversial topic.

Article solicitation: Board members soliciting articles from colleagues can be the eyes and ears for new writing talent for the publication from within the industry.

Board Function

The range of what members of an editorial advisory boards do is broad, as the survey results show:

Percent-of-respondents	Function of board members
88	Provide ideas for articles
83	Provide ideas for publication direction
73	Act as information source
67	Discuss industry issues
60	Contribute articles
56	Attend editorial advisory board meetings
47	Act as source for article quotes, direct and indirect
43	Identify article contributors
38	Provide manuscript consultation

Continued

Percent-of-respondents	Function of board members
34	Conduct peer reviews
27	Promote publication to readers
24	Discuss publication design
22	Guest edit an issue
20	Select contest winners
16	Answer reader questions
16	Fact check
16	Discuss readership studies
16	Nominate candidates for awards
14	Explore revenue-generating ideas
12	Discuss publication marketing
11	Discuss advertising of publication
8	Promote publication to advertisers
7	Discuss circulation
6	Make final decision on manuscript suitability
4	Critique issues
2	Give interviews to promote publication
1	Speak at conferences

Board Composition

How large a board is and who sits on it ranges widely for trade publications, anywhere from a few people to 20. Most boards are about the size of a typical focus group, between seven and 12 people:

Percent	Number of board members
40	7–12
22	20+
20	6 and under
15	13–15
3	16–20

Who chooses the board? It's usually the editor, but not always. In about three-quarters of the cases, the editor has all or part of the responsibility for board selection. But in the other quarter, it's others who select the board, and the editor has no input.

Percent-of-respondents	Board selection
41	Editor
33	Editor and either the publisher, editorial director, or existing editorial advisory board members (and in a rare case, the advertising director)

Continued

Percent-of-respondents	Board selection
9	Executive (for association publications)
6	Publisher
3	Existing editorial advisory board members
3	Board members and publisher
1	Advertising staff
4	Others

Frequency of meetings and compensation of members also figure into board structure. Most publications schedule a meeting at least once a year, but more frequent meetings are not uncommon.

Frequency of meetings

Percent of respondents	Scheduled meetings
39	Once a year
23	Once every other year
20	Twice a year
18	More than twice a year

Compensation

For most board members, compensation isn't an issue. Few publications offer payment, and where there is payment it's often to compensate for specific tasks such as manuscript review or article authorship. In cases where board members are compensated, the amount ranged from $400 an issue to $14,400 a year, although the figures aren't considered representative.

Readers and Advertisers

Of the publications that have boards, 46 percent have only readers as board members, 37 percent have "non-readers"—consultants, analysts, academicians, "industry experts," association members, and others, 16 percent have both readers and advertisers, and 2 percent have advertisers only.

Are Boards Necessary?

Many publications operate effectively without an advisory board and indeed many editors prefer to operate independent of a board, for a number of reasons.

For an editor who's trying to build expertise within the staff, an advisory board can be an impediment, at least if the board's relationship to editorial staff isn't managed effectively. Without that effective management, writers may rely on board members to the point of excluding others in the industry, neglecting the cultivation of sources from different standpoints, and lessening the imperative for the writer to master the subject matter.

"We are positioning our editors as knowledgeable experts," one editor says. "An editorial advisory board detracts from this somewhat. We already confer with a number of people in the industry for information and article ideas."

The concern is that reliance on board members for expertise can become a crutch.

"If you work the phones, do the research, and are involved in the industry, editorial advisory boards are not necessary," says an editor.

The desire for independence is strong among some editors, and there's a concern that that independence is at stake with boards whose members come with their own agenda.

"Most editorial boards we've seen are padded, or at least sprinkled, with representatives of the publication's biggest advertisers," says an editor. "In researching the idea several years ago, we asked industry leaders and public relations professionals their opinions; the response was not encouraging. Editorial boards were seen as mere wallpaper to be ignored, as 'window dressing,' not as needed advisers."

For some editors, the input of board members can seem like an encroachment on their turf.

"All of a sudden board members think they've got all this power and control over what you should publish and how you should publish it," an editor says. "They're like homeowner associations."

Nor are boards seen by some editors as having the right sense of what belongs and what doesn't belong in a publication. Knowing their industry isn't a substitute for knowing what's appropriate for publication and how it should be approached journalistically.

"We're a news-analysis-driven publication in which the main factor in our decision-making is news value to readers," says an editor. "Journalists are considered better able to decide what belongs in the publication than are industry professionals."

Given these hurdles, the amount of effort it can take to motivate board members and the cost and time in setting up meetings can seem more than what you get out of it. "A lot of work with limited payback," as one editor puts it.

Why Editors Like Editorial Boards

From finding story ideas to providing editors cover when they approach controversial topics, editorial advisory boards can play a key role in shaping a trade publication's content. Here's what editors said in a 2003 ASBPE survey on the subject:

✔ "We are a trade medical publication. Many of us do not have formal medical or scientific training or education. Our editorial board helps to ensure that our articles are factually and scientifically accurate."

✔ "We used to have an engineering editor. He retired. We couldn't hire someone quickly and lost the position entirely. The board helps fill that role. The board, which we doubled in size in the past two years, has been a tremendous resource for contributed editorial and peer review. They're among the best in the industry and are committed to our magazine."

✔ "As the only editor at my magazine, having a group of folk to bounce ideas off of is great. Additionally, our combination of industry experts and end users adds an additional element of respectability to our content."

✔ "Deeper insight into the information needs of our core readers, as well as more targeted critiques of the work we're doing than we can get from reader surveys or casual conversations with our sources/readers."

✔ "Members of the board provide insights into our industry that enable the writers to include nuance and subtlety in their writing that readers can't find elsewhere."

✔ "They act as a good sounding board, especially when we're considering delving into areas we haven't tried before."

✔ "It gives independent credibility by having these respected names in the publication, and they are an objective eye keeping us on our toes."

✔ "Brings you closer to your readership and helps avoid mistakes in terms of editorial direction. As the partnership strengthens, they take a vested interest in seeing us succeed and provide valuable feedback and help set or validate strategic direction."

✔ "Our advisory board represents the different audiences of our publication, and helps us stay on track with offering pertinent and beneficial editorial, suggesting 'hot' topics and providing firsthand perspectives."

✔ "Political benefit: The editorial board may be willing to 'sign off' or approve an article for publication whereas association staff (the magazine is published by an association) might have reservations about the article."

✔ "A really good dinner once a year."

Why Editors Don't Like Editorial Boards

In the view of some editors, boards aren't for every publication. Enterprising editorial staff that maintain wide-ranging contacts within an industry can stay on top of key industry issues without a board, saving the time, expense, and effort to maintain one. Here's what editors said in the 2003 ASBPE survey on the subject:

✕ "We have a circulation of just around 5,000, and only two editors. We just don't have the staff to even manage or interact with such a board."

✕ "Our publication is very horizontal, and to be representative of our market, the board would have to be quite large."

✕ "Our articles are based on reporting, not technical "how-to" information, so no need for peer review."

✕ "Our magazine informally solicits content from many facets of our industry. Our editor and the president of our trade association review content to maintain the appropriate message to our readers."

✕ "It's too difficult to find independent experts who aren't already working with or for industry manufacturers or distributors."

✕ "We work with many experts in the field, with whom we seek input. We build credibility by having these experts author columns. As a news magazine, the publication surveys its readers constantly to make certain editorial is well targeted. We have maintained our top readership standing in the profession for the last 16 years."

✕ "We review articles in house for relevancy to our readers, and we send them to one or two additional freelance technical writers for their opinion if needed. We feel as though we get the ideas and feedback we need without having an official 'board.' "

✕ "We find sending editors to various conventions of our market niche works quite well to obtain an industry pulse."

✕ "Our company prefers that our staff determine the magazine's editorial content. We do regularly contact industry professionals for opinions on topics we are considering or researching, but we do not have a formal board."

✕ "I don't believe that advisory board members are always sufficiently motivated to perform their advisory role properly, and an advisory board could be cumbersome to work with."

continued

✗ "We have a large staff of professional journalists who have specialized in this industry for years. They all are very connected to our readers and suppliers in the industry. We attend all the major meetings and conventions, and many of us are active in industry organizations. We get our feedback through our reporting and attendance at functions."

✗ "Our editorial is rarely technical enough to require a board."

✗ "With an editorial staff of 23 journalists, we have the breadth and depth to cover the subject without needing advice, guidance, counsel, whatever from outside experts. Also, we are a newspaper, not a journal."

✗ "Editorial advisory boards tend to limit the people you talk with. As subjects vary and change, you are more likely to find the best person to talk to based on the specific need rather than a board member who may or may not understand the area of the subject you are writing about."

✗ "We feel that advisory boards can sometimes become overtly political and tend to thwart the free flow of information that may be contrary to the conventional thinking or ways of doing things. Editorial advisory boards can become bureaucratic and bogged down if some individuals do not respond quickly."

✗ "Editorial advisory boards often want to serve their best interests, and not those of the industry or the magazines. It's human nature. If you get the wrong person on your editorial board, you can find your magazine getting into real trouble. I think if you work the phones, do the research, and are involved in the industry, editorial advisory boards are not necessary."

✗ "A lot of work with limited payback. Not enough financial/time resources."

✗ "Our editors are fairly specialized and have many years experience in our subject material and our readership. We feel we know the readers' needs fairly well. Creating a formal advisory board, we feel in our own case, would add political and other complexities that would be time-consuming without a significant up side. We periodically revisit the question. In the meantime, we have wide-open informal channels with many of our readers. We do get a steady stream of input."

✗ "We have weekly staff meetings with our information and legal team at which we discuss upcoming issues and hot topics for our members. There doesn't seem to be a need for a formal advisory board. This group seems to perform many of the functions of an advisory board."

✗ "Such a board is useful if the editorial staff is not expert in the magazine's field, or if there is no expert oversight in topic selection or editing. In our case the level above managing editor is expert in [the industry], and we are in touch with the field and our readership on a daily basis. In effect, our exec team performs the functions of an editorial advisory board."

The Editorial Advisory Board That Saved a Magazine

In the following interview, Michael Klim, former editor and associate publisher of *Trusts & Estates*, talks about how an editorial advisory board helped turn around the fortunes of the magazine.

Sherman: *Why did your publication have an editorial board?*

Klim: Sometime prior to my tenure at the magazine, the publication lost its editorial direction. Management decided to revamp the editorial advisory board and move the content of the magazine more in the direction of reader service and away from advertiser-influenced content.

To that end, the editor at the time conducted a search for an individual in the business who had the influence and the stature to impose on colleagues, to "cause to be produced" articles of sufficient quality to interest subscribers across the broad spectrum of trust and estate planning issues and draw them back into the magazine.

Such an individual was found. Not only was he well recognized in the industry, but he was willing to bring to bear his efforts and those of his firm (also well known in the business) on a pro bono basis. This person became the chairman of the editorial board.

Sherman: *How was the board set up, and did it represent your readers' interests?*

Klim: The advisory board would best function, it was decided, if it represented the broad readership in microcosm. An outstanding individual was sought in each area of expertise the magazine hoped to address (in this case, the legal, trust banking, accounting, investment, family office, sales and marketing, and retirement benefits professions) to be a part of the board and to "cause to be produced" articles for the magazine in their individual areas of expertise. It was further decided that the workable number of board members should be 13.

The board chairman advised on each monthly issue of the magazine. Each month, the magazine would focus on one area of expertise, with the board member in that area of expertise serving as the primary consultant for that month.

Readers would feel that at least one member of the board had their best interest as a reader in mind. Readers had a representative on the board that they could relate to, communicate with and perhaps submit articles of interest and ideas through.

The magazine would also include other articles and columns in other areas of reader interest to insure that there was something of material interest for every reader, every month, but there would be a primary theme with one editorial board member in one area of expertise in charge every month.

continued

The board was formed and the editorial calendar was set: twelve members (plus the chairman), twelve months, twelve areas of expertise, twelve themes, plus additional articles and columns every month.

Sherman: *How did the board operate day to day?*

Klim: Once the editorial calendar was set (in July for the forthcoming calendar year), board members knew for which month they were responsible. Four months prior to the date of publication, the editor would send a letter reminding the board member of the responsibility and setting a time in the near future when plans for the issue could be discussed.

At least three months prior to the date of publication the editor would call the board member in charge to discuss what issues in their particular area of interest were "hot" and who might author articles on these issues. Oftentimes, the board member would make the initial contact with these authors. Sometimes, the board member would just suggest topics and potential authors and the editor pursued these leads.

The editor would then track the progress of the individual authors to ensure that they were staying focused on the subject matter and that they would complete the article on time.

Two months prior to the date of publication all articles were to be received by both the editor and the board member. Both reviewed the articles and made final suggestions in preparation for publication.

In addition to their responsibility for a particular month, editorial board members reviewed and critiqued unsolicited articles in their area of expertise, solicited articles in any area of the magazine's coverage areas, acted as liaisons between the readers and the magazine's editorial staff, occasionally represented the magazine at trade shows and conferences, and examined additional potential revenue streams for the magazine.

Editorial board members were expected to be on call for the editorial staff.

Sherman: *So, the editor's role included one of being the chief coordinator?*

Klim: Yes, making sure that all the board members worked together in synchronicity for the month and the year to produce timely, well-written articles that would peak reader interest. As with most groups of individuals, some members were more cooperative than others and some were willing to contribute more than others. It was my job to solicit the best efforts from each individual and ensure that they conformed to the goals of the group as a whole.

continued

Sherman: *What exactly was the role of the board chairman?*

Klim: The editors of the magazine drew on his influence and expertise to provide editorial direction and quality content for the magazine. He was to make sure that other members of the board were responsive to the editors.

Sherman: *What did the board do at meetings?*

Klim: The board generally met for half a day at a central location. The first part of the meetings was spent discussing "hot" topics in general and then specific hot topics in each area of the magazine's interest. Board members were assigned a particular month on which they would be primary advisor. New areas of potential interest and possible direction of the magazine were discussed. Readership studies were examined, as well as ways to address changing reader demands. Upcoming trade shows and conferences were discussed including what support the board members might lend to the magazine at these conferences. General revenue figures were discussed. New areas of potential revenue were explored.

Sherman: *How often did you have meetings?*

Klim: Formal meetings were once a year, but impromptu meetings happened at most trade shows and conferences.

Sherman: *How were members selected?*

Klim: The estate planning and wealth management business is relatively small. New members were selected from the network of existing board members. Interest in serving on the board was first solicited informally from an existing board member and then formally, in writing, by the editor.

Sherman: *How long were people on the board?*

Klim: Members of the board served at the discretion of the editor and the board chairman. When they were unproductive, disinterested or nonresponsive, they were dismissed. Sometimes a change of focus in the magazine or a new area of concentration would demand that some existing members were dismissed and some new members were brought on to keep the magazine "fresh" and vibrant. Every new member was informed of this going in and it rarely caused any problems.

continued

Sherman: *What were some of the problems?*

Klim: In an ego-driven business, populated by highly educated, somewhat maverick individuals, working with board members was often like herding cats. In a business such as wealth management, "ego management" was one of the problems I faced. There were also frequent "political battles" with some of the law firms and banks that might have developed into publication of biased, poor quality editorial had I let it.

Sherman: *What did having a board do for the magazine?*

Klim: With this group of highly qualified, well-respected experts functioning as the editorial board—driving the review and production of timely, expert articles on important areas of interest to our readership, the magazine came to be known as the "bible" of the business. It was a "must read" for anyone in the profession. The magazine was *sine qua non* in the business. As a result, we often operated at a 90 percent market share with intense reader loyalty and virtually 100 percent paid subscriptions.

Taking the Tough Road

Lisa McTigue Pierce

Maryfran Johnson, editor-in-chief of *Computerworld*, doesn't kid around when it comes to editorial ethics. The newsweekly Johnson works for, owned by International Data Group, outlines 15 rules in its Editorial Code of Ethics governing the conduct of editors, including in their contacts with advertisers. The last item states, "Willful violation of any of these rules is grounds for disciplinary action, including dismissal."

How seriously do management and editors take these rules? "Completely serious," says Johnson.

When it comes to editorial ethics in the trade press, editors are in the hot seat. At the very least, the trade press, with its tight relationships between readers and advertisers, is vulnerable to charges that dollars, rather than journalistic enterprise, dictate editorial content.

The reality is more complicated, of course. There are surely publishers that allow some measure of advertiser influence. After all, one of the key functions of the trade press is to keep professionals in an industry informed about the latest product and services available to them. So, for publications that rely on advertising revenue to stay afloat, the path of least resistance for editors can mean the one that takes them through favorable coverage to advertisers.

But, as Johnson makes clear, a serious attitude toward ethics doesn't stop at the door to the trade press. How many consumer publications have published their editorial code of ethics in the pages of their magazine? *Computerworld* has, and readers praised it for doing so. "Readers can be your best defense," says Johnson.

That said, the pressure is clearly on trade press editors to compromise.

Studies show a high demand for trade publication editors to publish "advertiser friendly" articles, and that demand rises as the economy falls.

Laura Watilo Blake, a graduate student at Kent State University, conducted a nationwide Internet survey of business press editors in April 2003 to measure perceived advertiser and business pressure on editorial content. When asked "How often have you produced stories that may please an advertiser based on internal pressure in the last year?" 12.3 percent of 81 respondents said "Frequently" (i.e., 60 percent or more of the time); 30.9 percent said "Occasionally" (between 10 and 60 percent of the time);

Lisa McTigue Pierce is editor-in-chief of Food & Drug Packaging, *a publication of Stagnito Communications, Deerfield, Ill.*

and 56.8 percent said "Seldom" (10 percent or less of the time). More than 43 percent said they prepare advertiser friendly articles more than 10 percent of the time.

This isn't how it's supposed to work. Companies buy ads in a magazine because they want to reach specific readers and the quality of editorial creates the right environment for their marketing message. Editorial integrity and credibility bond readers to the magazine and make them want to read. If readers suspect that the articles are dressed up promotional copy for advertisers, they'll stop reading. You'll lose their trust. No readers, no audience. No audience, no advertisers. No advertisers, no magazine.

What Kind of Pressure?

The pressure to influence editorial content can take many forms. Just knowing how much money is at stake is a form of pressure. "The most insidious kind," says Johnson.

Can business press editors serve two masters—readers and advertisers? Many are trying because they're being asked to. According to Watilo Blake, results from her survey show that "editors are extremely conscious of the potential erosion of journalistic values due to increased advertiser and business influence."

Survey respondents identified the top consequences of advertiser influence on editorial content: credibility problem with the reader, 68 percent; financial concerns taking precedence over quality, 57 percent; and erosion of journalistic standards, 54 percent.

"Advertisers continually want as much free ink as possible, and they increasingly expect it," says one editor participating in the survey. "The ad sales department reinforces the sense of entitlement by selling primarily against editorial mentions, rather than for the overall editorial package or the reader community."

If you give in, it gets worse. What you do for one, you have to do for all, as many seasoned editors who replied to Watilo Blake's survey have learned:

"Once you start allowing the influence, you have to do it more and more to make up for the first instance," says an editor. "There will be no end to favoring advertisers in turn to make things 'fair.'"

Who Sets the Tone?

The root of the problem isn't pressure from advertisers. Editors pinpoint the real issue: a lack of internal support for editorial integrity and independence. That's why *Computerworld's* aggressive stance against ethical transgressions is key.

"Without backing from your publisher, there is no choice but to have to give in at times," one editor says. "I fight this vigorously, and am probably known as a bit of a hot-head about it. But I figure I am protecting the integrity of the book, and, as a direct result, the long-term sales."

It's not that editors are adverse to advertising sales—quite the contrary. Editors hope revenues will grow so they'll have more pages to publish the articles they know they should, as well as the ones they want to. And everyone wants to be part of a success. But sales and editorial departments often have different ideas on how to get there.

"We should be working together for a common goal," says one editor. "Too often the salesperson's goal is to please the advertiser and the editor's goal is to serve the reader. If these goals are contradictory, the [arguments] can seriously damage the staff's working relationship."

Can sales and editorial work well together without compromising editorial integrity? Yes, say several editors, especially when editorial staffs are small or inexperienced. Editors may even rely on salespeople to be their eyes and ears out in the field, talking with clients and potential customers. Do they ever pass along useful information for an article, though? Rarely, says Johnson at *Computerworld,* because they're looking at it from the vendor's point of view, not the reader's. But that doesn't mean they can't work together.

It may be hard to convince magazine salespeople that editorial integrity serves their advertiser clients better than caving in to their requests for free editorial. But it does, because it keeps the readers reading the magazine—articles and ads.

Beyond the Ad/Edit Issue

For trade press editors, advertiser influence is in many respects the largest ethical issue we face. It's certainly the ethical issue many of us spend the most time on. And the influence can happen in so many ways:

Contacts with editors. Advertisers contact editors directly with the intent of influencing content.

Gifts to editors. Advertisers provide promotional gifts to editors with the intent of raising their visibility for editorial consideration.

Payment of travel expenses. Advertisers pay to bring editors to a facility or event with the intent of generating coverage.

Joint editorial/advertising calls. Magazine sales and editorial staff participate in a joint call to an advertiser, the editor to get information for an article and the salesperson to build the relationship with the advertiser.

But ethical issues extend beyond advertiser influence on magazine content. These issues are the same as for the consumer press, and in many ways the consumer press is under more of a spotlight on them because of their wide visibility. Among the issues:

Contacts with public relations specialists. Here a company, agency, or individual is looking for favorable editorial coverage for a product or service.

False or misleading coverage. We've all heard the tales of fraudulent or biased reporting:

- Reporter Jayson Blair resigning from *The New York Times* in May 2003 when he was confronted with evidence of frequent acts of journalistic fraud. He admitted that he made up information and quotes, stole material from other newspapers and wire services and lied about where he was when he filed articles. Two of his senior editors also quit in the subsequent turmoil.

- NBC News firing reporter Peter Arnett after he gave an interview on Iraqi TV during the 2003 Operation Iraqi Freedom in which he criticized U.S. policy. Arnett apologized for his "misjudgment" and then later retracted his apology.
- Writer Janet Cook returning her 1981 Pulitzer Prize for "Jimmy's World," her article about an 8-year-old heroin addict that was published in *The Washington Post* in September 1980. Cook admitted that the story was fabricated rather than reported.

Resolving Issues

Without a doubt, at some point in your career you'll face an ethical dilemma, and it may be gut-wrenching. What to do? Here's what veteran trade press editors say:

- Argue your point until you convince others not to do what you feel is wrong. Logic, persistence, and your powers of persuasion can make this option work.
- Find a compromise. Think of at least one alternative that will satisfy everyone.
- Argue your point but give in to keep your job if you can't convince them not to do it.
- Threaten to quit if they force you to do something against your ethics—and then quit if they don't back down.
- Threaten to quit if they force you to do something you don't want to do—but then don't quit. You can only play this card once. And when you do, you'll lose more than just that argument.
- Don't even threaten. Just quit. That may slow them down before they try to push the next editor around.

How many of us could afford to quit without having another job lined up? But if your name is on an article or on the magazine's masthead, how can you afford *not* to quit if your reputation is at stake?

Johnson says that she would resign rather than compromise editorial integrity. On the other hand, Andrew Mykytiuk, editor of *Flexible Packaging* magazine and a colleague of mine, freely admits: "I would rather have a paycheck than a reputation."

Although it may be uncomfortable to oppose our superiors, we must defend editorial integrity. Johnson reflects, "You can't just have ethics when it's convenient. You've got to stick by these things even when there's trouble." And, sometimes they push you just to find out where that line is.

"If they don't know where that line is, it's your place to tell them," says Casey Bukro, co-chair of the National Ethics Committee of the Society of Professional Journalists. "It's tough to confront your boss or superiors, but sometimes that's what it takes."

If your company or magazine has its own Code of Ethics, learn them and live them. They can keep you from getting burned when advertisers or salespeople turn up the heat. If you don't have a Code of Ethics, consider writing your own or adopting one or all of the guidelines from the associations mentioned earlier.

Resources

For editors searching for answers to ethical issues, resources exist. Here's just a few of them:

Code of Preferred Editorial Practices, American Society of Business Publication Editors (*www.asbpe.org*). Helps identify potential ethical conflicts and encourages a high level of professional behavior. Full disclosure: I worked on a revision of the Code in 2000. At that time, magazine Web sites and online articles were under scrutiny, so we added a section to the Code on Web sites and electronic newsletters.

Guidelines for Editors and Publishers, American Society of Magazine Editors (*www.asme.org*). Sets a standard for editorial independence from "untoward commercial or other extra-journalistic pressures," and aims to ensure that the "clear distinction between advertising and editorial content is never blurred."

Code of Ethics, Society of Professional Journalists (*www.spj.org*). Originally adopted in 1926 and updated regularly. "Instructs journalists to seek truth and report it, minimize harm, act independently, and be accountable." The preamble explains that "the goal is not to provide all of the answers or settle all of the disputes but to help equip journalists to make clear, defensible decisions."

Code of Ethics and Guide to Preferred Practices, American Business Media (*www.abm.org*). "Provides a universal set of guidelines formalizing the high standards to which we all are held."

Conversation

Ethics On the Line

You're working for a small publishing operation, and you have no other editors to talk to about an ethics problem you face. Or maybe your situation is particularly complex or requires confidentiality. It may be helpful to talk things over with an unbiased third party, maybe even someone who's an expert in ethics. It was with these kinds of situations in mind that Ethics AdviceLine was launched in 2001 as a partnership between ethics specialists at Loyola University in Chicago and the Chicago Headline Club, a chapter of the Society of Professional Journalists.

Ethics AdviceLine works like this: journalists who are struggling with an ethical situation can request assistance by phone (312/409-3334) and receive a call-back from an ethics specialist within 24 hours.

What makes AdviceLine a bit different from other journalism hotlines is that the people who answer the phone are experts in ethics—not journalism. So they're able to step back and look at the big picture—at least, that's the aim. The AdviceLine team is made up of people who undertake ethics work in the business community, where practical solutions are crucial, and people who do ethics work in the academic sector, where the focus is on theory.

Staffing the hotline with ethicists was a deliberate decision, says David Ozar, one of the principals of AdviceLine. "If a journalist finds another journalist on the line, they're not going to feel like they're getting anything special." Ozar is a professor in the Department of Philosophy at Loyola University and director of the Loyola Center for Ethics and Social Justice, a non-academic service center connected to the college.

In mid-2003, I spoke with Ozar and Casey Bukro, also a principal of Advice-Line, on the problems and the solutions discussed over the hotline since its launch. Bukro is the ethics chair for the Chicago Headline Club, a chapter of the Society of Professional Journalists, and co-chair of SPJ's National Ethics Committee.

How Does AdviceLine Work?

The role of the counselor at AdviceLine is to take you through the thought process so you can arrive at the answer yourself. Bukro says it's similar to what he calls a "doping" session, where you verbalize what you think a story is about. It forces you to organize your thoughts. "Once a person articulates what the problem is, they begin to see the solution themselves or at least understand the situation more," he says.

Seeing the situation clearly and knowing how to react to it are two different things, though. By talking with someone who is an expert in ethics rather than another journalist, callers get a more impartial look at the issue. "It's the equivalent of another set of eyes and ears," says Ozar. "The broader the base of experience

continued

that your judgment is resting on, the more likely you are to come to some kind of wisdom."

Ozar doesn't always know how the situations turn out because counselors don't follow up with the callers. "We just give our advice and hope it goes well," he says. Is it hard not knowing the rest of the story? "Yes and no," Ozar says. "First, those of us who answer the phone aren't journalists and so probably we don't have as much of an itch to know what happened as you would. The other part of it is that it's extremely important, to do this right, that you have a strong sense of the privacy involved. A reporter's curiosity is in some sense the opposite of protecting privacy."

AdviceLine seems to be working. After more than two years, Ozar says the service is getting reasonably good at helping journalists help themselves. "When you think about ethics all the time, you get articulate about what the questions are and how to word some of the concepts," he says.

Questions often involve conflicts of interest, relationships with news sources, and weighing the harm that might come from reporting a story. "If I had to pick one thing that journalists that I've talked to over these two years are most clearly sensitive, it's when the personal relationships and journalist relationships clearly conflict," says Ozar.

Ozar shares some examples: Can you date someone that you're writing about? Can you consider a job offer from one of your industry sources? The easy answer is, yes—but you better not be writing about them at the same time. And, what do you tell your boss if he or she asks you to do an article about them?

Of the calls they get, about half are from people asking legal questions or strategic questions about their careers, or from people who want to know more about AdviceLine. The other half deal with substantive ethical issues. "Very often, we get people wondering if what they thought was right, is right," says Bukro.

But that doesn't mean that callers are asking only simple ethical questions. "I'm impressed at the sophistication of the questions we get," says Ozar. "But we are fairly certain we haven't reached the smaller shops. Big organizations have big pressures but even the little organizations have what are correspondingly big pressures. At least in the big organizations, there's someone to talk to. We have a feeling that the people [who] may be the most needy for someone to talk to, we haven't regularly reached. Our challenge is to figure out how to get the word out."

Bukro says that he's seeing more education, training, and sensitivity to editorial ethics, but it's still a drop in the bucket to what's needed. "I would love to be able to say 'We really understand the ethics implications and we're really sharp on this stuff and isn't journalism grand?' but I cannot tell you that," says Bukro. But ethics can be taught—and should be taught. Journalism schools cover the basics: dealing with conflicts of interest and weighing harm vs. benefit. But those lessons won't reach the trade press editors whose background isn't in journalism but in

continued

the industry they cover. We assume they know to stay as impartial as possible, but sometimes they don't.

Yet these editors are on the front lines. "I think, more often than not, ethics is driven from the bottom up," says Bukro. "We don't give the working stiffs enough credit for being sensitive to it. This is growing because we talk to each other and we realize, just by looking at the news, that these issues are important in the way we work and in our futures—because a bad operation just doesn't last. That's part of what we can do to maintain the vigor and health of any place we work for is to be sure that we're watching for things that don't seem right. That's everybody's job."

See chapter exercise at the back of this book.

American Society of Business Publication Editors

Code of Preferred Editorial Practices
Revised November 2000

This Code of Preferred Editorial Practices is not intended as a mandate, but as a practical guide for members of the American Society of Business Press Editors (ASBPE) and the business publication editorial community in general. We hope this Code helps identify potential ethical conflicts and encourages a high level of professional behavior, practices and policies.

ASBPE urges its members to maintain the highest ethical standards. It believes that editors should be aware of the confidence, trust and responsibility placed in them by their publications' readers, and do nothing to abuse that obligation. At all times, editors should avoid any practice that would serve to compromise or appear to compromise their objectivity, fairness, and balance.

I. Contacts with Editors

Communications from outside sources on editorial matters should be addressed directly to editors, not through or to anyone else.

Editorial decisions should be made only by the editorial staff. Proposed articles, comments, suggestions or complaints should be evaluated independently by the editorial department, which should reach a decision based on editorial considerations alone. Any other procedure inevitably leads to bias and allegations of bias, and thus threatens the editorial integrity of the publication.

Input from sales personnel should be weighed with a view to overall fairness, but should not be allowed to overly persuade. Nor should their input be allowed to override an editorial decision.

Editors should be sure advertising sales personnel understand and support this direct contact policy because it frees them of the constant pressures that may be directed at

them by advertisers. To insist that customers deal only and directly with editors on editorial matters protects both the publication and its representatives in the long run.

II. Gifts to Editors

As a rule, editors should not accept gifts from editorial information sources or advertisers. Gifts can be a source of embarrassment to the editor and publication receiving them, and editors should discourage the practice. One easy-to-follow guideline: If you can't eat it, drink it or smoke it in an hour, don't take it.

As in most fields, however, business gifts are an established custom, making the practice difficult to avoid completely. Following are some guidelines to help judge individual cases:

1. Modest, souvenir-type gifts commonly given to attendees at a press affair are generally acceptable.

2. Modest gifts sent to a large number of recipients are generally acceptable.

3. Money or lavish gifts sent to a single recipient or to a select few are generally not acceptable. Acceptance of modest gifts sent to a single recipient is questionable, but the decision rests with the individual and/or the publication.

4. Acceptance for personal use of "samples" or gifts of items or products that are (or may be) the subject of editorial mention is questionable. Depending on your industry, however, samples may be accepted if they assist in your understanding of the product or article subject — for example, review copies of books or software — but should be returned.

American Society of Business Publication Editors

The following guidelines outline preferred procedure:

1. Public relations personnel can be requested to assist in arranging contacts with key personnel at information sources.

2. When an article idea originates in a public relations department, it is logical to seek further details from this source.

3. When additional interviews are needed, public relations can assist in making appointments and advising on appropriate personnel at their client company.

4. Public relations is the logical source for suitable illustrations and company clearance when needed.

5. When articles involving a given company originate outside the public relations department they should be cleared with public relations if there is any possible doubt about company figures, quotes or other factual details.

6. When advertising and public relations responsibilities are vested in the same individual, a clear distinction should be maintained between the two functions. Editorial material should be evaluated only on the basis of its information or educational value to readers. An advertiser or potential advertiser should not be entitled to preferred treatment.

7. An advertising representative of the publication is not a good substitute for an editor at press announcements or in the collection of editorial material. If he or she is so used, he or she should be careful not to use the occasion to solicit advertising.

8. Editors should always reserve the right to report or not report on a press get-together.

9. Editors can use their own discretion on whether advance copies of an article should be previewed and/or approved by sources or individual subjects of that information. An exception may be made when it is allowed for purposes of verifying and/or checking the accuracy of technical information. Propriety, courtesy and common sense are urged when making the decision.

VII. Web Sites/E-mail Newsletters

On all such pages, editors should ensure that a clear distinction is made between advertising and editorial content. This may involve type faces, layout/design, labeling, and juxtaposition of the editorial materials and the advertisement.

Editors should directly supervise and control all links that appear within the editorial portion of the site.

VII. Advertising/Advertising Supplements/Advertorials

Editors should not write, edit, design or otherwise create any content for advertisers or advertising sections.

However, editors should help ensure that advertisiements and advertising sections do not take on the "look" of editorial. If necessary to further ensure that there is a easily visible distinction between editorial and advertising via labeling or design.

Overall Editorial Practices Policy

Editors are urged to use common sense, businesslike thinking, professional behavior and practices and, last but not least, let their consciences be their guide.

**American Society of
Business Publication Editors**

III. Payment of Travel Expenses

The term "travel expense" includes transportation, lodging, meals and personal expenses.

Generally, editors should not accept payment of travel expenses incurred in the course of performing editorial duties from any source other than the magazine itself.

There can be exceptions to this rule, however. Two of the most common are:

1. In the case of group press affairs attended by editors from more than one publication, if the offer to pay expenses is extended by the information source to all participants, acceptance of payment is optional. Also, in the case of group press affairs, it is common practice to accept free transportation chartered or operated by the information source.

2. In the case of travel to fill speaking engagements either at an association or company affair, acceptance of payment of travel expenses is optional.

IV. Outside Activities of Editors

Editors should not undertake any outside employment or enter into any paid or unpaid association with advertisers, editorial information sources or readers that in any way could result in conflict of interest. Following are typical cases to serve as a guide.

Editors should not undertake outside work that:

1. Could reflect unfavorably on the editor's publication (as when he or she is asked to write for an outside publication statements that conflict with the views of his or her own publication);

2. Is done for a competitor of his own publication;

3. Is done for a public relations or marketing department of a company or for a public relations, marketing, or

advertising agency for use as the product of that department or agency;

4. Is what an editor properly owes to his or her own publication, as when he or she accepts an outside writing assignment on a subject that would be a logical assignment for his or her own editorial pages.

V. Joint Editorial/Advertising Calls

Joint calls by editorial and advertising sales personnel should be made only under prescribed conditions. The following procedures are preferred:

1. Under no circumstances should advertising space be solicited by an editor during a joint call.

2. When an editor accompanies advertising sales people, he or she does so to explain or interpret editorial policy. For example, he or she can explain the publication's editorial objectives, the nature of its audience, trends and problems that exist in the field the publication serves, evidence of editorial usefulness to readers, and future editorial projects.

3. When an editor accompanies sales personnel on visits to advertisers or potential advertisers, it is acceptable for the editor to collect material for specific editorial projects. The editor should conduct research on specific articles alone and separately, however.

4. Joint calls should not be made to answer or discuss complaints on editorial matters. If, during the call, complaints do arise on editorial matters, these should be handled solely and directly by the editor.

VI. Contacts with Public Relations Personnel

It is common practice for editors to work with or though public relations personnel. Public relations people, however, should not be allowed to influence opinion, interpretation or presentation of an article. Nor should they be allowed to preview the article prior to publication.

EXERCISES

Name _____   **Date** _____

Exercise
Chapter 2
Publication Launch
Think Like a Publisher, Create Like an Editor

The Business Plan—Develop Your Own

A business plan is usually necessary to win support from senior management. Remember that a business plan serves two purposes: 1) organizing your thoughts and ensuring that all aspects of a magazine launch are considered, and 2) giving management confidence by describing what to expect and when.

A simple, straightforward plan of a few pages should have a table of contents something like this:

Executive Summary
Introduction
    Industry Trends
    Opportunity for New Publication
    Competitive Environment
Magazine Description
    Mission and Competitive Advantage
    Audience
        Readers
        Advertisers
    Editorial Content
    Sales
    Marketing
    Circulation
    Production/Distribution
Related Franchise Opportunities
    Web and Email
    Conferences or Tradeshows
    Buyers Guide
    Newsletter
    Other (e.g., collaborations, cross-marketing)
Pro Forma Statement (details of expected expenses, revenue, and timeline)

Using as a guide the issues explored in the *WDM Solutions* case study and the sample business plan outline above, develop a plan for launching a business publication targeted to a niche audience.

NOTE: Tear out this Exercise sheet and hand in with your completed business plan.

Name _____   **Date** _____

Exercise
Chapter 3
Editorial Direction
The Well-Defined Redesign

Is This Publication Ready for a Redesign?

Review the content and design of a business publication from the standpoint of its intended readers. The journal section in your library should have a fairly large selection if you're not familiar with or don't have access to a business (business-to-business) publication. Review three issues at a minimum, then provide a critique (both good and bad) of how well content and design elements are working for the intended audience. Explain why elements are or are not working, and how you might change elements that aren't working. In your critique, consider the following points:

Publication facts. Name of the publication, circulation size, mission statement, last time it was redesigned (if you can tell by looking at back issues).

Intended readers. Who are they, and what kind of publication can they be assumed to prefer (i.e., in-depth text with focus on analysis, not graphics or how-tos; quick-read articles with lots of how-tos and diagrams of how things work; emphasis on visuals with fine graphics)? To help you, look at the publication's editorial mission in the masthead. Also, determine the audience advertisers are trying to reach.

Cover. Is the tone of the cover appropriate to the readers (technical, pretty, serious, light, etc.), and does it look professional?

Table of contents. Is it easy to find articles? Do you have a sense of what an article is about without having to turn to the page?

News. Is the news written and its presentation designed to grab attention, help readers, and give a picture of what's happening in the industry?

Departments. Are column topics clear right away? Are the columnists and their topics well matched for the readers? Are they appropriately in-depth?

Features. Is there a range of article topics that covers different aspects of the industry? Is there a mix of different types of feature such as how-to, trend, profile, issue analysis, etc.?

Overall design. Does the presentation of articles and the use of graphics, colored backgrounds, and fonts match the character of the readers?

NOTE: Tear out this Exercise sheet and hand in with your critique.

Exercise
Chapter 6
Technical Editing I
Turning Experts into Writers

Assigning an Article to a Subject-Matter Expert

Create an assignment for an article on the latest innovations in bicycle derailures for an audience of bicycle store owners. The writer is the lead engineer at AAA Bicycle Manufacturing. Key points to consider in making the assignment:

Audience knowledge. What is the level of knowledge about derailures that bicycle store owners can expect to bring to the article? Given their expected level of knowledge, what information should the writer assume the audience already knows, and what is the new information?

Audience interest. What should the article focus on in light of the readership of store owners? In what way would the focus differ if the readers were bicycle manufacturing engineers or bicycling enthusiasts? What is the primary interest of store owners in new derailure technology?

Author bias. As an engineer at AAA Bicycle Manufacturing, the author can be expected to draft an article that showcases technology innovation at her company. If her company was the only manufacturer of a certain derailure technology, it may be appropriate for her to showcase her company's products. If there are other manufacturers with comparable technology, how should the author approach the topic?

Presentation. What are key design considerations for a piece of this type, and how might those considerations differ for an audience of bicycle engineers or of enthusiasts?

NOTE: Tear out this Exercise sheet and hand in with assignment.

Exercise
Chapter 7
Technical Editing II
Tough on Facts, Easy on Words

Rewriting an Original Submission

Review and rewrite the draft article entitled "New Directions in the Apparel Industry." Take an approach different from the version rewritten as "Natural Fibers: The Eco-Friendly Alternative." Consider the intended readership for the piece, which includes executives in the decorative apparel industry, which markets printed T-shirts, among other products. Some points to consider:

Main point. What is the central piece of information the author wants the reader to obtain? How might other points in the piece be organized to support this principal objective?

Reader knowledge. What knowledge about the global textile industry does the readership likely bring to the piece, and in what way should the article build on that knowledge?

Take-away value. What information from the draft can be highlighted, possibly as a sidebar, to provide as much professional benefit as possible to readers?

NOTE: Tear out this Exercise sheet and hand in with assignment.

Exercise
Chapter 11
Feature Planning
A Cool, Deep, Nourishing Drink

Covering an Issue Comprehensively

As editor of a trade publication for pharmaceutical company executives, you plan to devote an upcoming issue to a crucial problem in your industry: the high cost of drug development. To showcase the problem, you would devote your entire feature well—four stories—to the issue. You'll also approach the topic in other parts of the magazine. Among other things, you'll ask a columnist to write about some aspect of the problem, and you'll focus your lead news story on federal government action that impacts the cost of drug development.

Below are issues associated with drug cost development and a partial list of different types of features. In the space provided, suggest how you would cover some of the issues. What mix of features would you use, and what types of features would you use to cover which aspects of the problem?

Keep in mind that, in a typical feature well, there is a cover story and one or more secondary features of different types. Your aim is to devise a mix of features that your readers could view as a resource for them in addressing their own problems with high drug development costs.

Issue Points

1. The creation of prescription medications is a costly and drawn out process subject to intensive research, adherence to exacting protocols, complex clinical trials, and heavy government regulation.

2. There have been some particularly difficult and expensive drug developments recently.

3. Drug companies use different methods for financing trials for drug safety and effectiveness.

4. Technology companies have developed products such as electronic diaries for patients to increase the efficiency of drug trials and thereby reduce the cost.

5. Despite the challenges the drug industry faces, there have been cost-effective drug developments.

6. The industry has many researchers who've made a leading contribution in making drug testing more cost effective.

Feature Types

1. Company or individual profile

2. Best practices

3. Investigative

4. How-to

5. Trends

6. Human interest

7. Product

Name _____ **Date** _____

Exercise
Chapter 16
Editorial Ethics
Taking the Tough Road

Ethical Dilemmas for Editors

As an editor of a business publication, you face issues that raise questions of editorial independence, the appropriate editorial-advertiser relationship, among other matters of journalistic ethics. Consider the scenarios below, choose one, and outline how you would handle the situation from your perspective as an editor. For purposes of the scenarios, business publications include scholarly journals and magazines (including Web publications) with links to an association.

Conflict of interest. You commission an article from a freelance writer you haven't worked with before. She turns in the article on time, and exactly as specified. Just prior to sending the issue to your printer, you discover that she has received a payment from a public relations firm hired by a company that makes a product that is a focus of the article. Do you publish the article?

News embargo. At a large international medical conference, a researcher announces that a commonly used drug for a serious medical condition is, in fact, ineffective. You prepare a news report for your magazine, and call the researcher for an interview. He tells you that, because pre-publication release of his data could jeopardize publication of his article in the New England Journal of Medicine, you may not reference the data that was presented at the meeting, even though press were invited. The researcher threatens that, if you publish the article, you will be unable to interview other researchers at his institution, one of the country's leading centers for medical research. The ineffectiveness of the drug is unknown to the general public, though millions of consumers are taking it. Do you publish your article?

Advertiser pressure. You receive a letter from the agency representing a major brand of drug. The letter states that it must be notified in advance of any mention of the drug in your publication, positive or negative, and that it reserves the right to with-

Questions used with permission of Peter Banks, publisher, American Diabetes Association, Alexandria, Va., developed for the Society of National Association Publications 2003 national conference.

draw advertising based on the nature of the mention of the drug. If you fail to notify the company of a product mention, it reserves the right to a full make-good on the ad. Do you accept the advertisement under these conditions?

Advocacy conflict. You publish a peer-reviewed journal. The director of your government relations department complains that a recent research article in the journal reached a conclusion at odds with the association's advocacy efforts. The director demands to review all articles published in the journal, and to prevent publication of research that contradicts the association's positions. The editor of the journal, who is at a university, says the integrity of the journal is at stake, and he will resign if there is any interference with the peer-review process. What do you do?

Association conflict. You cover a conference for an association publication. At the conference, a researcher who is an officer of your association speaks, and you prepare an article that quotes her directly. You confirm the accuracy of the quote from your tape recording. Prior to publication, the researcher calls and insists that she be allowed to edit her remarks so that they more closely align with the association's. You object to changing direct quotes, and offer to paraphrase her or attribute the quotes to a later interview. However, the author insists on editing her direct quotes. What do you do?

Sponsor pressure. One of your association's largest corporate sponsors has just signed a multi-year multi-million dollar sponsorship agreement. Your development department insists that the president of this company be featured on the cover of the magazine. In the past, you have always avoided profiling any one sponsor, for fear of appearing to endorse this sponsor's products and services. Do you go ahead with the cover profile?

Sales staff review. Your new advertising director insists on reading the contents of the entire issue prior to publication so that he can contact advertisers whose products and services are mentioned and sell ads based on the mention. Do you agree to this practice?

Ad positioning. The same advertising director does sell an ad based on the mention in the magazine, but the advertiser insists that the ad may only appear if it is positioned adjacent to the article mentioning the product. Do you agree to position the ad in relation to related editorial?